D0897741

Africans of Two Worlds

Africans of Two Worlds

The Dinka in Afro-Arab Sudan

Francis Mading Deng

New Haven and London, Yale University Press

1978

Published with assistance from the Mary Cady Tew Memorial Fund.

Designed by John O. C. McCrillis and set in Journal Roman type.
Printed in the United States of America

Published in Great Britain, Europe, Africa, and Asia (except Japan) by Yale University Press, Ltd., London. Distributed in Latin America by Kaiman & Polon, Inc., New York City; in Australia and New Zealand by Book & Film Services, Artarmon, N.S.W., Australia; and in Japan by Harper & Row, Publishers, Tokyo Office.

Library of Congress Cataloging in Publication Data

Deng, Francis Mading, 1938-
 Africans of two worlds.

 Includes index.
 1. Dinka (Nilotic tribe)—History. 2. Sudan—Politics and government. 3. Dinka (Nilotic tribe)—Politics and government. I. Title.
DT133.D54D46   962.4   77-76305
ISBN 0-300-02149-6

To my son
Daniel Jok

Our blood . . . was one with our hyenas, with our leopards,
with our elephants, with our buffaloes; we were all one . . .
we are one people . . . we should all combine—the people,
the animals, the birds that fly—we are all one. . . . Let
us all unite . . . even the animals that eat people, even the
people who keep the black magic that we do not like,
let's embrace them all and be one people.

—Chief Makuei Bilkuei

Contents

Foreword

I have long considered Francis Deng to be part of a new generation of African leadership, which after being inspired by liberation struggles is now providing leadership toward development. Dr. Deng, who is both statesman and scholar, can rightfully take pride in his contributions toward the historic development of his country—the Sudan.

Dr. Deng has added yet another noteworthy accomplishment to his long list with his latest book, *Africans of Two Worlds: The Dinka in Afro-Arab Sudan.* It is a deeply moving and human chronicle of his people and the prospects of their peaceful integration into the Sudan.

One of the most intriguing parts of this latest work is Dr. Deng's utilization of oral history. I am sure Dr. Deng is familiar with the studies of Dinka society produced by western anthropologists, historians, and former colonial administrators. He could have taken the easy route and used these studies as his reference point. However, Deng chose to base his book upon his own extensive interviews with a number of chiefs, who were asked for their views on the history of their people. In a broader sense, Dr. Deng's book illuminates the problems Africans are facing in retaining their own values while building independent political structures viable in the modern world.

I got some amazing insights into the dynamics of the Dinka culture by reading Deng's work. I only wish that there were more scholarly works of this nature that reflect the perspectives of the people who know their history and aspirations best.

I firmly believe that when we begin to understand what is important to other people and what is their long-range concern for the future of their nations we learn that there is a common ground upon which all humankind might build a peaceful existence.

Dr. Deng once told me that, although the Dinka people number over two million and are by far the largest ethnic group in the Sudan, they are among the most significant Africans least known to the outside world. I agree that I too once knew very little about the Dinkas, but thanks to Dr. Deng I feel that I have had a very intimate encounter with the Dinka people.

ANDREW YOUNG

Preface

The oral material from which this book has been prepared provides unusual insights into the perspectives of Dinka chiefs and elders about the past, present, and future of their people. The material is presented through a policy-science methodology that reflects the inside view of the Dinka while maintaining an observational standpoint that considers the wider national and international contexts of their present-day and predictable future involvement. The book is interdisciplinary in approach, welding together mythological, historical, sociological, political, and developmental aspects of Dinka experience as an integrated composite whole, a portrait of Dinka cosmology.

The Dinka are a Nilotic people in the Democratic Republic of the Sudan whose closest national kindred are the Nuer and the Shilluk, but they form part of the ethnic and cultural complex that involves all Luo-speaking peoples, extending into the neighboring countries of East Africa, with physical resemblances that are visible in the Masai of Kenya, the Tutsi of Rwanda and Burundi, and as far west as Mali and Senegal. Tall, lean, and blackest of the dark races, they present something of an anomaly, with features that reveal non-Negroid elements and an origin that remains obscure, despite the observable similarities across the continent. Numbering nearly three million in a country of less than twenty million inhabitants and over five hundred tribes, the Dinka are by far the most numerous ethnic group in the Sudan. They are among the wealthiest Africans in livestock, with a traditional economy dominated by cattle and, to a lesser extent, goats and sheep. But while their devotion to cattle has tended to overshadow their agricultural occupa-

tion, they are also keen subsistence farmers. Spread over a
topography that is segmented and not infrequently flooded
by the Nile and its tributaries, the Dinka have been relatively
isolated even from one another, glorying in their race, their
land, and their wealth. Their ethnocentric and conservative
orientation, reinforced by the preservative policies of British
colonialism, have given them a reputation of resistance to
change and cross-cultural assimilation. Post-colonial trends
have, however, revealed not only their adaptability to chang-
ing conditions but also their potential for making dynamic
contributions to the building of a modern nation-state. Their
long history of agonizing struggle for survival against alien
invasion and aggression is now faced with the positive challenges of peace, unity, and cooperation in an extended community of man.

The goals of the book are to promote "essential knowledge" of the Dinka by revealing salient facts necessary for
the enlightened formulation of policies, to be realistic in the
selection of alternative models in the light of the complexities of national and global interaction, and to be scientifically
positive in recognizing and building upon those features in
the experience of the Dinka and their compatriots which
provide constructive bases for creatively molding a modern
nation from the enriching diversities of human experience.

The book is divided into five sections including the Introduction and the Conclusion. After introducing the Dinka, the
Introduction raises and discusses in broad terms a number of
substantive issues arising from the themes of the interview
material, recognizing national unity as an overriding goal that
is not only nationally postulated but regionally and internationally sanctioned. The achievement of peace between the
Arab North and the Negroid South and their present relations
in an atmosphere of harmony are viewed as providing constructive foundations for unity and the predicted integration,
as well as a raison d'être for another look at the history of

South-North relations with a view to facing courageously the realities of the post-civil war period, in order to avoid past mistakes and even correct them, and to recognize the positives and build upon them.

These themes are elaborated and developed in three substantive chapters. The first, "The Origin of Things," deals with what is largely a mythical history of the Dinka, starting from a conceptualized beginning at the Creation, remembered and retold in great detail through creation myths that are linked with the legends of original leadership and early migration. The reader may find this chapter disproportionately long, but quite apart from their intrinsic flow and classic value, which discourage summarization, these myths reveal some of the most deeply rooted principles that underlie the highly spiritual, religious, and moral outlook of the Dinka. The striking parallels between these Dinka myths of creation and the biblical or Koranic versions, with such themes as Adam's rib, the snake, the Garden of Eden, the fruit of temptation and the like, indicate that there must have been some South-North contact and cross-cultural influences predating the more recent contact with Christian missionaries which occurred during the British colonial era of the twentieth century. This early process, of which only an assimilated substantive evidence remains in Dinka religious tradition, accounts for the similarities which anthropologists have observed between Dinka religion and the Middle Eastern religions, and should contribute to the bridging of the cultural gulf between the South and the North—a gulf which has been exaggerated but which is now narrowing with the increasing realization of the African component of the Afro-Arab integration of the North.

The second substantive chapter, "Contact with Outsiders," covers three historical phases. The first, the pre-Condominium era, includes the earliest unrecorded contacts, which are accounted for only in mythology or in vague historical conceptions, and extends to the nineteenth-century Turko-Egyptian and Mahdist regimes, which did not bring the Dinka fully under their control but which brought them into contact with waves of slave raiders, whom they recall as Turks, Egyptians, and Arabs without making clear distinctions. The second phase is the Anglo-Egyptian Condominium, which came at the end of the nineteenth century and was the first foreign power to successfully establish colonial rule over the Dinka. Because it ended the terrorism of prior systems and permitted the Dinka to govern themselves through indirect rule, it disguised its colonial yoke and became appreciated as protective and virtuous. For this reason, independence, which marks the third phase, was received ambivalently by the Dinka, as bringing freedom to the country but introducing the threat of domination by the North and a possible return to the disorder of the "spoiled world" of the nineteenth century. The mutiny which broke out in the South a few months before independence, later followed by a civil war that lasted for seventeen years, proved that their fears were justified.

The third and last substantive chapter, "Building the Nation," concerns itself with the post–civil war period that began with the Addis Ababa Accord and the enactment of the Southern Sudan Provinces Regional Self-Government Act in 1972, giving the South regional autonomy within national unity. Unity not only became the common call of both the North and the South, but is also universally hailed as one of the most outstanding achievements of the May Revolution. The consolidation of the achieved peace through the uniting ideology of equitable social and economic development has become a national preoccupation. Considering the peaceful and harmonious, though cautious, interaction that now characterizes South-North relations, and the verbalized commitment to national unity as an overriding consideration, the Sudan may be said to have entered a new phase of predictable integration with which the third and last substantive chapter ends.

The Conclusion restates the major themes of the Dinka heritage, stressing the depth of past suffering, animosity, and bitterness, but contrasting them with the remarkable achievement of peace and the apparent acceptance of unity as an overriding postulate, indeed an achievement to be preserved at all costs. The recognition and consideration of the sentiments of the Dinka as expressed by the chiefs and elders are viewed as vital to any corrective solutions that can realistically guarantee lasting peace and facilitate nation-building. The views of the chiefs and elders on the future of North-South relations range from suggestions of specific changes required in the attitude of the North as prerequisites for full and lasting unity, to a basically skeptical preference for a wait-and-see approach, and to an even more pessimistic prediction of eventual, mutually agreed or violent, separation. These views, which are largely circumscribed by traditional outlook, are appraised in the wider context of national, continental, and international commitment to the preservation of the present boundaries and the fostering of broader loyalties. With these formidable constraints, quite apart from the inherent value of unity, it is reasonable to assume that unity and eventual integration are not only desired goals but predictable outcomes of these overriding considerations, especially in view of the present institutional arrangements with the osmotic effect of their regional-national stratifications.

The equitability of unity and integration cannot, of course, be precisely quantified, but judging from the present discrepancies, more input from the South would be required to achieve adequate balance. Unless such balance is achieved a functional consensus cannot be fully guaranteed. In order to maximize the South's contribution and broaden its support for unity and integration, a strategy is postulated whereby divisive concepts of national identification are scrutinized, uniting concepts are substituted, and an integrating approach to economic, social, and cultural development is advocated. Such a concept of nation-building is envisaged as potentially enriching the Sudan with the immense resources of its ethnic and cultural diversities, and in turn reflecting a representative sum-total which all citizens can identify, glorify, and take pride in as collectively "Sudanese," while utilizing its African and Arab components in a creative and dynamic manner to serve national, regional, or international objectives of mutual interest to the Sudanese peoples of both the South and the North.

Acknowledgments

Although the collection and processing of the data in this book began in 1972, I have been concerned with the study of various aspects of the Dinka since 1959, when I conducted my first field research into customary law among the Ngok Dinka. In a more subtle and less formalized way, my interest in Dinka culture goes back to my childhood and involves a long chain of people who would be impossible to enumerate.

While fairness to all may require mentioning none, I cannot refrain from expressing exceptional appreciation to some. Foremost are of course the chiefs and elders whom I interviewed and whom I consider the real authors of the book. I hope that having kept my pledge for publication is sufficient tribute to their contribution. May it give them and their posterity an increased sense of pride in what they said and in the heritage of the people about whom they spoke. I am also grateful to Arthur Akuien, now member of the People's Assembly, and Andrew Wieu, former Minister of State in the Presidency, who were instrumental in arranging the meetings with many of the chiefs and who shared the objectives of my research.

A grant I received from the International Legal Center of New York gave my research encouraging recognition at its initial phase. I am especially indebted to Professor Yash Ghai, then Senior Fellow in the Yale University Program of Law and Modernization and an Associate of the International Legal Center, whose understanding and support were instrumental.

A number of friends and relatives have read the manuscript, assisting with proofreading or contributing useful observations. In particular, Professor Robert Collins, for whom the history of the Southern Sudan has been a subject of major academic concern, made invaluable contributions to the improvement of the manuscript and was one of the principal promoters of its publication. I am also indebted to Professors Yusuf Fadl Hassan, Mohammed Omer Beshir, and Herman Bell, not only for their substantive comments on the manuscript but also for their interest and support, which led to the involvement of the University of Khartoum as co-publisher of this volume and publisher of the texts and translations of the interviews. K. D. D. Henderson, former Provincial Governor in the Anglo-Egyptian Condominium and author of several books on the Sudan, and Hassan El Tayeh Abashar, then Sudan Cultural Counselor in Washington, also read the manuscript and made valuable and encouraging comments. Lawrence and Robert Ludwig, together with other members of the Ludwig family, assisted with the proofreading and substantive revision of the manuscript when time was crucial. I also received editorial assistance from Isobel Clark, then with the Institute of Afro-Asian Studies of the University of Khartoum.

An invaluable contribution was that of Christina Diss, who transcribed the translation tapes and typed and retyped the manuscript in its early stages. Edith Adams-Ray, Evelyn Hernandez, Gigi Cesario, Janice Ezeani, Manju Vanjani, and Salome Tantoco all assisted in the typing of later versions.

A special word of appreciation must go to Marian Ash of Yale University Press, who, by combining firm editorial objectivity with encouragement and support, gave me a challenge that proved a very constructive contribution to the value of the book.

From the conception to the completion of this work, my dear wife, Dorothy, has been a close partner, assisting in recording the interviews, contributing to the development of the methodology, acting as a sounding board for my ideas on matters of detail, and otherwise rendering unfailing support, encouragement, and faith.

1. Introduction

Issues

On March 27, 1972, after long, intensive, and discreet nego-
tiations, the Sudan announced the successful conclusion of
the Addis Ababa Accord, ending a civil war between the
Afro-Arab North and the non-Arab South that had devastated the country and frustrated economic and social development for seventeen years. With that resolution, which granted
the Southern people an autonomous status within a united
Sudan, Africa's most chronic, but by no means unique, conflict became the first and so far the only peaceful solution of
an ethnic conflict on a continent permeated by diversity,
rivalry, and, not infrequently, violent confrontation. The
settlement was universally hailed by regional and international organizations, governmental and nongovernmental. Nevertheless, that the agreement was at all possible after such a
long, bitter, and indecisive war was almost unbelievable. Not
even the optimists could be sure the settlement would last.
It has now been meticulously observed by both sides for over
five years and can be safely said to have so far succeeded.
Since the agreement, a positive mood has emerged in South-
North relations which must necessitate a reexamination of
the divisive concepts that have dominated political thinking
on the relations between the North and the South. Divisiveness has tended to overemphasize the profundity of racial
and cultural dichotomy, the depth of animosity and mistrust
resulting from an embittering history, and impediments to
any hopes for solidarity in nation-building.

So predominant did the adverse view resulting from the
presumed racial and cultural dichotomy become that myth
overshadowed reality. The obvious racial and cultural ad-

mixture of the North and the similarities between Southern and Northern peoples became blurred by the simplistic vision of the North as racially and culturally Arab and religiously Islamic and of the South as Negroid and pagan. A more detached view of the situation would show that, both in color and features, the North contains visible Negroid elements, existing separately or integrated with the Arab elements. There also exists in the Northern Sudan abundant evidence of non-Islamic, non-Arab, African cultural elements which have survived the Arabization and Islamization or Afro-Arab integration the North has undergone. This is true in both urban and rural areas, but it is particularly striking in the tribes where pre-Islamic languages, dance and song styles, and even attitudes toward the role of women in the economic and social life of their communities have survived. Even societies which have been exposed to Arab cultural influence from the earliest period, such as the Nubians and the Beja, show remarkable resilience in the degree of cultural continuity. The Fur and the Nuba of the western Sudan are more racially and culturally Negroid than Arab, and many of the Baggara, while known for their pride in Arabism, reveal obviously Negroid features. As a people, they are well known for their pre-Islamic attitude toward women and their vigorous African dance rhythm, not to mention the dominance of cattle in their economy, from which they derive their name.

All this is the recognized outcome of the eclectic method by which Islam spread in the North, a process not at all peculiar to the Sudan, for Islam has been known throughout its various epochs to accommodate the preexisting ethnicities and cultures and promote itself on their indigenous bases. In many parts of Islamic Africa, outward rituals of fanatic devotion are recognizably embellished by the underlying strength of the prior religion of the people. Even the new forms of religious expression often contain rituals and practices that are clearly pre-Islamic.

Conversely, it has also been observed that many Southern peoples reveal non-Negroid racial and cultural elements. In their *Pagan Tribes of Nilotic Sudan*, the Seligmans argue that the Nilotics have Hamitic Caucasian elements in their admixture.[1] The late Professor Sir Edward Evans-Pritchard also observed that "It is doubtful whether any people in the Sudan can be regarded as true Negroes and their non-Negroid characters, their pastoral pursuits, and, to a certain degree, the structure of their language are attributed to Hamitic admixture and influence."[2] Trimingham has noted that "It is rare to find anything approaching a pure racial type among any of the peoples of the Sudan, for this land has suffered many events of racial dispersion. All its people are variations between the pure Caucasian and the pure Negro type. So the black skinned people of the South are usually referred to as Negroids [instead of Negroes]."[3] In his study of Nilotic religions, Professor Evans-Pritchard observed that the Nuer and the Dinka show closer resemblances to the classic religions of the Middle East than to traditional religions of Negro Africa. The presence of pyramids in Nuer- and Dinkaland is an obvious evidence. The burial rites of the divine chiefs of the Dinka have also been characterized as indicative of ancient Egyptian rites. Early Egyptian paintings show bulls with horns curved in an unusual manner; they resemble the curves resulting from the Dinka and Nuer practice of training the horns from an early age to grow in a shape suiting the owner's taste. Indeed, one does not have to dig into the distant past to substantiate the thesis of cultural linkage with

1. 20 (1932). See also C. G. Seligman, "Some Aspects of the Hamitic Problem in the Anglo-Egyptian Sudan," *The Journal of the Royal Anthropological Institute of Great Britain* 93 (1913):610-42.
2. Edward Evans-Pritchard, "Ethnological Survey of the Sudan," in *The Anglo-Egyptian Sudan from Within*, ed. J. A. de C. Hamilton (London, Faber & Faber, Ltd., 1935), p. 88.
3. John S. Trimingham, *Islam in the Sudan* (London, Frank Cass, Ltd., 1949) quoted in *Peace and Unity* (Khartoum, Ministry of Foreign Affairs, 1973), pp. 16-17.

the North and the Middle East. Contemporary research in cantometrics (song style) and choreometrics (dance style) indicates that the Nilotics do not easily fall into the Negroid African cultural group but instead reveal a combination of the African and the Middle Eastern styles.

The adoption and assimilation of the concept of the Mahdi in the late nineteenth century is an obvious example of the dynamic process of cross-cultural influence that must have occurred. Indeed, the Turko-Egyptian and the Mahdist periods in the Sudan had left such a profound religious and cultural influence on the more accessible peoples of the South that the implementation of the British policy of separate development initially aimed at de-Arabizing and de-Islamizing the South. Southerners were encouraged to abandon Arab-Islamic names and modes of dress and to avoid speaking Arabic which had then emerged as the lingua franca of the region. Even after the policies of separate development had left their mark on the South, striking evidence of Arab-Islamic influence remained, especially in urban areas. What is known as Juba Arabic today, an adapted form of Northern Arabic, has so spread throughout the South that it is the lingua franca of the region, and English, which the British had intended to replace Arabic, has remained the language of the educated elite. Indeed, the Dinka and the Nuer seem to have been more remote from these late nineteenth-century Arab-Islamic influences, so that any evidence of racial and cultural admixture with the North among them must imply an even greater influence among the more accessible peoples near urban centers or close to the Nile routes.

The degree of racial and cultural admixture in the Sudan is perhaps best demonstrated by the 1956 population census which divided the Sudanese peoples into the following percentages: Arab, 39; Nilotic, 20; Fur, 9; Beja, 6; Nubiya, 6; Nilo-Hamitic, 5. The same census revealed that Arabic was spoken by 51 percent of the Sudanese population, Nilotic languages by 18 percent, and Northern Central Sudanese languages by 12 percent.

These indications of racial and cultural admixture have been observed but have not found acceptance in the attitudes of the people, which have been molded by the bitterness of recent experience. The focus of recent history and popular conception has been on the mutual isolation of the South and the North and the violent upheavals which marked their encounters during the nineteenth century.

In many instances, the oral material reproduced in this book dramatizes the theme of dichotomy and diversity, but it also provides a wealth of information which throws considerable light on aspects of South-North relations that have been overshadowed by a negative disposition and preoccupation. For instance, the myths of the Dinka about God, creation, original leadership, and early migration strikingly confirm the observations of anthropologists about the close resemblance between the traditional religions of the South and those of the Holy Books and indicate that early contacts between Southerners and the outside world might have been more substantial than has been supposed. While the Dinka themselves do not consciously make the religious link, and their conception of the people encountered during their early migration is that of "spirits" or "powers," they provide detailed descriptions of their characteristics and mention recognizable areas that leave us with no doubt that their conception is a mythologization of the real world and, for that matter, the world to the North. Nor can there be any doubt that this information does not reflect a recent Christian or Muslim influence. After all, modern foreign religious influence among the Dinka came only toward the middle of this century, long after the Condominium rule had been established and other parts of the South opened to missionary activity. Most of the chiefs and elders who furnished the information are men in their fifties, sixties, eighties, and nineties and they all claim to have received the information from their fathers and grandfathers whose lives would surely predate the advent of modern Christianity into the area. Also noteworthy is the consistency with which these stories are told throughout Dinkaland, thereby showing the depth and uniformity of the cultural roots.

If the theory of South-North mutual isolation prior to the nineteenth-century hostilities is dismissed, it goes without saying that Islam, Christianity, and perhaps Judaism have been features of Sudanese civilization from earliest times and therefore evidence of these classic religions among the Southern peoples should not be surprising. The acceptance of ethnic, cultural, and religious linkage underlying the history of South-North relations should also mean that no clear-cut racial or cultural dichotomy can be drawn between the two parts of the country. From a policy standpoint, to see essentials in common and be able to realize that there is no profound difference of race or culture should enhance mutual respect and acceptance between Southerners and Northerners.

The process is already under way and may indeed have been a factor in the settlement of the Southern problem. Over the years, Sudanese on both sides have increasingly realized that the North is not as Arab and non-Negroid as had been thought, nor the South as non-Arab and Negroid as had been assumed. The North, indeed the whole Sudan, is now more appropriately referred to as Afro-Arab, a label that is less divisive or, to state it positively, more unifying. As the Sudanese begin to see more in common, racial and cultural barriers become less marked, the sense of superiority or of resentment at subordination becomes modified, and a spirit of unity in national identification is concomitantly fostered.

The challenge in this new context is to face the realities of past hostilities with moral courage, understanding, and

tolerance, to acquire a deeper insight into the agony of yes-
terday in order to appreciate better the magnitude of today's
achievement, and to formulate for the future a plan of action
that is enriched by correcting the past. Nor is this only an
academic theory; it can indeed be a widely shared perspective should the positive developments become firmly established in the people's consciousness. Dinka oral tradition
shows how pragmatic, dynamic, and policy-oriented man's
perception and utilization of history are. This cannot be
surprising, for history is a record of critical events which by
their very nature force the observer who feeds material to
the historian, and the historian himself, to take a value-posi-
tion. Such partiality need not be in the form of overt advo-
cacy or alignment; it may be implicit in the very fact of
material selection and presentation. This is not to question
the desirability of objectivity but to recognize the constraints and the potentials of the shortness of memory and
the positive creativity of·history.

Oral history tends to be less presumptuous in its claims to
objectivity than written history. And indeed oral history is
particularly remarkable in its flexibility and adaptability to
contextual purposes. Knowledge is passed on from generation
to generation and each recipient and transmitting generation
sifts, reinterprets, and projects what is in line with the prevailing currents of political thinking.

The creativity of history goes on and is adaptable even to
dramatic shifts in political situations. Two of the eleven
interview situations from which the material in this book
resulted were conducted among the Ngok Dinka of Southern
Kordofan on two separate occasions that show the degree
to which political events can condition historical perspective.
I conducted the first interview shortly after the civil war,
when the Ngok Dinka—being administratively in the North
and therefore excluded from the autonomy granted to the
South and from the programs of relief, resettlement, and

rehabilitation then operative in the South—were in a politically charged situation that was virtually unchanged in its
sensitivity, repression, and explosiveness. Their theme, from
myths of creation to speculations on the prospects of integration, was to stress the dichotomy between the Arabs
and the "Black Peoples," the distinctiveness of the Dinka
and their Southern kindred, and the impossibility of full
unity, far less integration, with the North. After some constructive steps had been taken to implement a form of
autonomy in the area (the Ngok people having taken charge
of local government, security, education, and development),
I conducted a second set of interviews and heard a complete
reversal in the themes. The Arabs and the Dinka were then
seen as having been created by God as one people with
language differences occurring later as a minor mishap; the
country was then conceived as having always been one and
united; and the situation of the Ngok on the South-North
borders was no longer seen as detrimental and isolated but
as a positive one linking, reconciling, and actively promoting
national integration.

This readiness to reexamine the situation in the light of
new developments also underscores another significant
observation which is substantiated by Dinka oral tradition
from the myths of origin to speculation on the future. Conflict is not a new experience to the Dinka but a recurrent
theme from which has developed a heritage of the people
displaying resilience and survival. To the Dinka, and this is
known to every child, the world has been "spoiled" many
times before, and it has "held" again and again. People will
die, perhaps in large numbers, but the land will remain,
generations will grow, and society will thrive again. Implicit
in this thriving will be the normalization of friendly relations
between feuding groups, warring neighbors, and all the
pivotal elements of the relevant world.

Some of the interviewed chiefs and elders indeed referred

to the long chain of hostility between the South and North as domestic quarrels between relatives, sometimes conceived in varied relational terms as sons of the same mother, sons of the same father but different mothers, or cousins. They thus bring to mind the sociological truism that the closer a relationship, the more likely and intense the conflict, and the greater the need for constraint and regulation. Within the family, so strong are the internalized constraints and supplementary informal sanctions that formalized regulations become unnecessary. Wider social circles require formal regulations, supplemented by internalized constraints and informal sanctions. Beyond the juridical circles, the maintenance of order between neighboring units becomes marginal, even though proximity continues to imply both the intensity of actual or potential conflict and the need for regulation and sanction. Dinka-Nuer relationship is a classical, though overemphasized, example in anthropological literature. South-North relations provide another model of conflict between peoples of close historical, sociological, and geographical proximity.

Notwithstanding the positive developments of recent years, it is too soon for the people of the South to say or pretend that they have forgotten. The nineteenth-century hostilities have become remote and could have been forgotten had divisive interests and further conflicts not kept the memory alive. Indeed, the sentiments of the chiefs and elders whom I interviewed on the issue of South-North relations were ambivalent. On the one hand, they are profoundly appreciative of the magnitude of the peace achievement, the humane principles behind it, the moral courage it required from the leadership, and the divine wisdom they believe must underlie a settlement that has brought enemies into brotherhood. Some even recognize that the change is bound to facilitate the process of integration. Their words of praise for President Nimeri, who personifies for them all the spiritual

and secular dimensions of this achievement, are normally
reserved to men whom the Dinka elevate to the realm of the
suprahumans, second only to the spiritual world in sanctity.
A number of chiefs argued that he could not be an ordinary
person begotten by an ordinary man or an ordinary woman;
he must be a son of God, conceived directly through God's
spirit operating in his mother's womb. Dinka mythology is
most likely to immortalize this sanctification, and indeed
it is under similar circumstances that such religious heroes
as prophets came into Dinka mythology

On the other hand, they also view the settlement as a pragmatic realization of the impossibility of imposing unity
on the South, and accept the present arrangements as a compromise solution that must be accepted at least for now; but
they remain skeptical about the prospects for lasting unity
and prefer to wait and see whether peace has really come,
whether the Northerners are sincere in their word, and
whether they will make the necessary adjustment to ensure
lasting peace and unity. Many chiefs likened the situation
to a wound which had been given medication and was under
observation to see if it would heal. Others went further to
say that even if it healed, a scar would remain and should
be protected from anything that might open the wound
again. Yet others held an even grimmer view of the future,
seeing the peace settlement as tenuous, the Northern change
of attitude uncertain, and the threat of renewed conflict
impending. The best safeguard, as they see it, is separation,
which should be mutually agreed but if necessary could be
fought for again.

As a result of these ambivalences, the reader may well
observe an apparent contradiction between my rather san-
guine appraisal and the accounts of the chiefs. On its face,
such an observation may appear valid, but a close examination of the Dinka situation, within the broader context of
which they are now a part, should reveal that the contra-

diction is more apparent than real. In this connection, a number of considerations should be elucidated.

First, there is no disagreement over the facts of past or recent history. The existing discrepancies concern only views of the future, whether as a matter of prediction or of postulation. In both cases, those interviewed, looking at the bitter history of past South-North relations, acknowledge the positive achievement of peace but do not see it as necessarily having laid a foundation for the future realization of full unity and integration. They find the wounds of past hostilities too deep and the Northern attitude too alienating for such a positive development to occur. Of course they are not fully aware of the other constraints which the world political scene places on separatism, whether through the commitment of the Organization of African Unity and all African states to the principle of national unity within the boundaries inherited from colonialism, or by the balance of the forces at work nationally, regionally, and internationally.

My policy-science orientation, on the other hand, is that, quite apart from any personal preference for unity, one must recognize the probability that Africa will not lend itself to separatist trends on the continent and that, whatever the justification or military strength of separatist movements, they can best be settled on the principles of autonomy or federation. I see such autonomy or federation as merely establishing the requisite harmonious atmosphere for the interaction of the diverse national elements with the prospects of eventual integration. To be acceptable, this postulated integration must be equitable, must emphasize unifying labels, and must aim at ultimately reflecting the sum total of all the interactive principles in the national process. This model of integration, which I have expounded in *Dynamics of Identification: A Basis for National Integration in the Sudan,* is both a postulation and a prediction based on a close analysis of the process of integration in the North, the

more recent trends toward the search for a common Sudanese identity with greater awareness of the non-Arab elements in the Northern ethnic and cultural composition, and
the increasing recognition and respect for the non-Arab
component in the South.

The Afro-Arab integration of the North, which predates the
advent of Islam but was intensified by the expansion of the
Islamic empire, is particularly revealing on both the appropriate conditions required for integration and the degree to
which certain symbols can be projected to favor certain
outcomes in the process of integration. After initial confrontation and conflict, peace treaties were concluded which left
the Sudanese virtually independent with only a remote
control by the Islamic empire. The Arab Muslim traders in
the Sudan thus settled and interacted with the Sudanese
under conditions of relative harmony and mutual respect,
but which favored certain Islamic and Arab labels as models
for mutual assimilation. Among the contributing factors
were the facts that the Arabs possessed greater economic
advantages and were considered more advanced by virtue of
their universalizing religion and culture. Intermarriage involved Arab men and Sudanese women, and the offspring
were identified with the Arab male line with all that such
identification implied of ethnic, cultural, and religious
assimilation. The advantages of this assimilation, contrasted
with the disadvantages of being a "heathen" and a potential
victim of slavery, favored Arabization over equitable Afro-
Arab integration. And, as I have already said, the conceptual
identification with Arabism far outweighed the factual
balance of the Afro-Arab components of the Northern
Sudanese identity.

But the northernization process in the Sudan and the
independence movement of Black Africa, combined with the
increasing pride in the African Negroid identity and greater
exposure to the complexities of racial identification on the

world scene, eventually led to a more balanced view of the Sudanese reality. In the United States, Europe, and indeed within Africa, the Northern Sudanese began to see people who were of even lighter skin than himself being referred to as "Negroes" and "Black." In the Arab world he found himself viewed as rather a marginal Arab, and sometimes even referred to as "slave," leading to greater identification with "African," "Negroid," or "Black."

The result has been usually an emotional reaction to the opposite extreme, but more constructively it has led to a greater awareness of the hitherto hidden elements of the Afro-Arab Sudanese identity. These considerations, combined with other contributing factors—not least the Southerner's determination to have his non-Arab identity recognized and respected, and the Northerner's persistent defense of the principle of national unity—helped bring about the peaceful resolution of the South-North civil war.

Recognizing the restraints now placed on separatism in Africa, and the value placed on the principle of broadened unity, which the chiefs do not see, my alternative policy position is to build positively on the foundation of unity and autonomy which the peace settlement has established for the South, within national unity. I view the peace and the acceptance of the principle of unity not only as past achievements but as creating conditions of harmonious but constraining interaction, somewhat comparable to those which had facilitated Afro-Arab integration in the North. The precise nature of the outcome is a matter of conjecture which I discuss in alternative terms in appropriate places in the book.

In order for this harmonious atmosphere to be maintained and reinforced, it is important for participants in general, and policymakers in particular, to understand the Southern view of the past, the suffering they have undergone throughout their remembered history, the bitterness they nurse as a result, their grim view of the prospects for the future, and the conditions under which better alternatives can be developed. While the chiefs and elders are rather pessimistic about the future, they not only recognize the positive achievement of peace, they also accept the imperative of unity as a fundamental, though doubtful, "must" and speculate on conditions that, if established, could ensure the continuity of peace, consolidate the achievement of unity, and help promote national integration. For instance, apart from advocating continued respect for Southern autonomy, the chiefs urge the North to contribute to the development of the South both as a demonstration of the brotherhood the Northerners claim exists and as a compensation for past wrongs. Another major condition for "real unity" and "national integration" which is unanimously voiced is that the North abandon religious discrimination over mixed marriages and indeed encourage such marriages as an effective way of breaking down the ethnic and religious barriers that now exist between the Northerner and the Southerner.

By pointing out the Southern views on the past, present, and future as far as it can be predicted, we hope to facilitate the understanding and therefore the harmonization of the interacting or conflicting interests of the Southerners and Northerners and thereby enhance the prospects for equity in the outcome of the predicted integration. It is through a reasonable satisfaction of the expectations and demands of the Southern people as articulated by their elites that a workable solution can be found to the impending problems of disunity which have impeded nation-building in the past, and may continue to threaten the present achievements and prospects for the future.

From the foregoing it is apparent that the process, though logically based, is part of a broader, more complex, situation in which many factors interact with far-reaching implications that fall outside the vision of the Dinka as represented by their chiefs. Nevertheless, that vision is vital both to understanding the past and present situations, and to making the appropriate adjustments for the future. Indeed, a distinction should be drawn between the chief's descriptions of past hostilities and their predictions of continued adversities. While agreeing on the former, we emphasize different aspects of the latter. My appraisal of the future is built on the logic of the present achievement, future constraints, and a positive search for constructive alternatives, while the chiefs' pessimism rests on past failures and a grim view of the prospects for unity. But neither the chiefs nor I can speak with certainty; we can only speculate and postulate. The fact that some chiefs say the South and the North will and should separate after five years shows the depth of suspicion and fear that must be considered and provided for, but it does not mean that the Sudan will in fact separate in five years. Quite the contrary, the opposite seems obvious. And yet the possibilities for the future remain ultimately unknown.

In his foreword to my book, *Tradition and Modernization*, Professor Harold D. Lasswell commented on the South-North problem that "acute civil strife is perhaps the travail that is required to consolidate more stable arrangements."[4] One can say in retrospect that the long indecisive civil war has ironically served this purpose, for it has shown the South the degree to which the North is committed to national unity and will fight for it at all costs, and it has equally demonstrated to the North that, unless recognized as an equal citizen of his country, the Southerner will not accept a unity imposed by the North in the primary interests of the North with the Southerners as second-class citizens. Each now seems to display a mutual respect for the other's position.

On this mutual ground there may be political controversy on details, but the major trend has been defined in a pre-

4. Francis Mading Deng, *Tradition and Modernization* (New Haven and London, Yale University Press, 1971) p. xix.

dictable form, whatever the views of individual or collective participants. National unity and equitable social and economic development seem to be uniformly agreed upon as rallying points.

This brings us to another era in which the accounts of the Dinka throw significant light on contemporary views about Southern peoples and especially the Nilotics, namely their supposed resistance to change. Anthropologists have consistently emphasized the racial and cultural pride of the Nilotics, especially the Dinka and the Nuer, their resentment to any outside interference, and their imperviousness to Arab or Western cultural influence. As I indicated initially, observers of contemporary Nilotic society are much more likely to be struck by their adaptability to modern conditions and their high achievement motivation in the modern context. Paradoxically, both those who overemphasize conservatism and resistance to change and those who are more struck by adaptability are correct. Self-respect, pride, and belief in their value system have been essential defensive weapons against the elements that have threatened their system with destructive change through the various phases of Southern history. Yet, these could not have been successful tools of construction or survival if the people had not been selective in their response to other cultures, adopting that which could enhance their strength, resilience, and survival, while rejecting that which would either weaken the system or add no significant value to its resources.

Unless explained, the reputation of the Nilotics as indiscriminately opposed to change or adoption from other cultures can only be a myth in view of the observable evidence to the contrary. Indeed, the cross-cultural assimilation and therefore similarities between the Muslim-Arab North and the non-Arab South could not have been possible if the degree of resistance to change or cross-cultural influence had been as strong as is alleged. The apparent resistance to change or imperviousness to foreign cultures which gave rise to the well-known myth of Nilotic conservatism must have been generated by a withholding of information about the outside by the British colonial administration. After all, the philosophy of British colonialism was to develop the South along indigenous lines and therefore to discourage the adoption of Arab-Islamic and even European ways as possible disintegrating influences. How could change be conceived in the abstract if, in the context, the policy and indeed the practice were to conceal the facts of change or present them with the clear indication that conservatism and respect for tradition were preferred models?

It was not until the barriers between tradition and modernity and between the different ethnic and cultural groups were broken down at the dawn of independence, and the opportunities for modernization and cross-cultural influence became available, that the potentials of the Nilotics to change, adapt, and develop became visible. They have since demonstrated their adaptability and cultural dynamics beyond doubt. In fact, what the chiefs and elders have to say on development goes beyond disproving the theory of their conservatism and resistance to change; it demonstrates in a potent and forceful manner the immense human and cultural resources that remain alert and ready for a full mobilization toward the ambitious goal of accelerated and broad-based agricultural development that the Sudan has set itself. Indeed, one of the most remarkable things the Sudan government has done has been to successfully utilize equitable development as a uniting ideology or strategy, which has effectively mobilized all forces including those for whom the end to the civil war might have left open a dangerous void. Development is now the constructive raison d'être of the whole country, including the traditional sector.

Dinka oral history tells us much more about the Dinka and their relationship to their neighbors and the world around them than we have been able to know from available records. The material in this volume gives this insight not only because of what the informants expresssly stated, and their opinions on that, but also what we can infer in the wealth of information they provided about Dinka mythology, the long chain of upheavals and survivals, and the more recent dramatic history of conflict, reconciliation, and cooperation. Dinka history is not simply one of suffering and bitterness, but also a record of survival and achievement—an unending chain of challenges, always leading to renewed vitality and a realistic but manageable view of the future. Placed in the context of national, regional, and global dynamics, with overriding commitments to national unity and broadening of loyalties, the material in this book not only provides essential knowledge on the expectations and aspirations of the Dinka that must be considered in consolidating peace and unity, but also reveals the creative potential of the people to respond constructively to the complex challenges of nation-building within the pluralistic society of modern Sudan.

Sources

This book is the product of largely oral sources with minimum reference to published materials. It is based on material collected from eleven interview situations involving sixteen chiefs and elders from nearly all major subgroups of the Dinka. Other persons were also present in the interviews and some of them contributed views from which I have occasionally quoted. However, their significance remains subsidiary to the material elicited from the principal contributors. In this section I have included brief biographical notes on these contributors and have made some general observations on the distinctive features of the material provided by each individual, the rationale for the choice of the chiefs as informants, and the degree to which they are representative of the Dinka as a whole. Nine of the interviews were with chiefs from major sections of the Dinka of the Southern provinces, while two were with chiefs and elders from the Ngok Dinka of Southern Kordofan Province, the only Dinka section administered as part of the Northern Sudan. Presented in a sequence of traditionals to modernizers, the Southern Dinka contributors included Chiefs Giir Thiik, Arol Kacwol, Makuei Bilkuei, Ayeny Aleu, Stephen Thongkol Anyijong, Yusuf Deng Ngor, Thon Wai, Lino Aguer, and Albino Akot Awutiak; while the Ngok Dinka contributors included Biong Mijak, Pagwot Deng, Bulabek Malith, Chol Adija, Loth Adija, Marieu Ajak, and Acueng Deng. Although the Ngok are "Southerners" like their fellow Dinka in the Southern provinces, and share their ancient heritage, their more recent political experience has peculiar features that render their situation somewhat anomalous, and distinguishes them from the rest of the Dinka. In the original manuscript I had a separate chapter on their more recent history, but I subsequently decided that it interfered with the flow of the general material on the Dinka. I therefore excluded it from the book and turned it into a separate monograph.[5] But since their myths of origin are included here, and passages on later periods occasionally quoted, I have included biographical notes on the inter-

5. Under the title of *Frontiers of Nation-Building: The Position of the Ngok Dinka in South-North Relations,* to be published by the Institute of African and Asian Studies of the University of Khartoum. The interviews themselves will also be published by the Institute under the title of *Dinka Cosmology.* My other books on the Dinka are: *Tradition and Modernization: A Challenge for Law among the Dinka of the Sudan* (New Haven, Yale University Press, 1971); *The Dinka of the Sudan* (New York, Holt, Rinehart and Winston, 1972); *The Dinka and Their Songs* (Oxford, Clarendon Press, 1973); *Dynamics of Identification* (Khartoum, Khartoum University Press, 1973); *Dinka Folktales* (New York, Africana Publishing Co. 1974).

viewed Ngok chiefs and elders along with the rest of the contributors.

The first contributor, the now deceased Chief Giir, otherwise referred to as Giirdit (*dit* being an honorary suffix meaning "senior"), who died only a few months after this interview, was a chief of the Apuk, a branch of the Rek Dinka of Bahr al-Ghazal Province. He was sometimes called Giir Kiro after his father's older brother who had died before marrying. Thiik married Giir's mother in Kiro's name according to the custom of "ghost marriages" whereby a man may beget and raise children in a deceased brother's name, thereby ensuring its continuity.

Chief Giir was a man in his nineties when the interview was conducted, but even twenty years earlier, Dr. Lienhardt, who had done part of his fieldwork in Giir's tribe, had observed of him, "There are few men of Chief Giir Kiro's age and experience whose memories remain so clear."[6] He was not only clear on tradition but was also very much at peace with it, despite the context of radical change in which he then lived and about which he was not naive.

The interview was recorded on August 2, 1972, in Wau, the headquarters of Bahr al-Ghazal Province, and in the house of Mou, the educated eldest son of the chief, who occasionally interceded in the interview. Also present at the recording were several visitors, among whom was a young man by the name of Akol Kwen, who also participated.

Arol Kacwol, Chief of the Gok Dinka of Bahr al-Ghazal, was in his seventies when the interview was conducted. Although he went through hard times during the civil war, and is reported to have been subjected to physical torture, he demonstrated a rare serenity and objectivity of approach, which could only be qualified, though possibly also ex-

6. Godfrey Lienhardt, *Divinity and Experience* (Oxford, Clarendon Press, 1961), p. 26.

plained, by his deep sense of religious devotion. The interview was recorded on March 1, 1973, in Juba, the capital of the Southern Region. Also present was Arthur Akuien, now Member of the National People's Assembly, who contributed significantly.

Makuei Bilkuei, Chief of the Paan Aruw Dinka of Upper Nile Province, was in his late eighties when I interviewed him. In a curious way, he welds something of integration into tradition with a sense of inward disharmony, which seems to emanate from the vexations of hard times. Often it was nearly impossible to follow what he had to say, even when he was unshakably certain of what he was saying, and he would be repetitive and consistent in formulating his remarks. This was, for instance, the case with respect to his questions about "the earth" of the South and whether it was fused with that of the North in one box or kept separate, a point which touched on the issue of unity and integration, and which seemed to highlight his vexations. The interview was recorded on March 4, 1973, at Juba in the presence of Arthur Akuien, who also participated.

Ayeny Aleu, a Rek Court President from the Jur River District of Bahr al-Ghazal, was about fifty to sixty years of age at the time of the interview. He combined cleverness and wit with unusual candor. His initial insistence that I identify my policy lines with respect to South and North before he would talk typifies his shrewdness in manipulating situations. As further evidence of his shrewdness, he was remarkably aware of the personality dynamics in the interview situation and often involved those present, by way of praise, to concomitantly advocate his own causes. The interview was recorded on March 1, 1973, in Juba, in the presence of Arthur Akuien, who occasionally interceded.

Thongkol Anyijong, a chief of the Atuot Dinka of Bahr al-Ghazal, acquired the name of Stephen when he became converted to Christianity. Then a man in his fifties, Chief

Stephen Thongkol Anyijong suffered gravely from the civil war disasters, which he recounts in great detail in the interview. Although he never went to school, his association with the educated, and his conversion to Christianity, gave him a political sophistication and involvement that eventually took him into exile in Zaire with other members of the Anyanya, the military wing of the Southern Sudan Liberation Movement. The interview was conducted on the same day and in the same circumstances as those of Chiefs Arol Kacwol and Ayeny Aleu.

After interviewing Chiefs Arol Kacwol, Makuei Bilkuei, Ayeny Aleu, and Stephen Thongkol separately, I again talked to them collectively, primarily to answer some similar questions they had posed separately, but also to prompt them to make new contributions with a distinctive and collective character.

Chiefs Yusuf Deng and Thon Wai, from the Bor Dinka, were interviewed together. They were then in their forties. Their expressed dedication to their responsibilities as chiefs and to their promotion of the relevancy of chieftainship to the society of today and to the challenges of development can justifiably be described as obsessive. While Yusuf Deng displays a degree of alienation from tradition, a fact easily discernible from his adherence to Islam, Thon Wai remains tied to tradition and displays an impressive knowledge of it. Both men were, however, part of an institution then threatened by the forces of change. Their preoccupation with the modern role of the chief, especially in promoting development, was clearly a self-defense aimed at establishing relevancy and legitimacy in the face of modern threats to chieftainship. The evidence they adduce about the perspectives of the chiefs objectively justifies their obsession and indicates the otherwise ignored potentials of the institution for the novel purposes of integrated transition. There were, however, distinctive features to their individual positions which justify their particular commitment to change. This was evident in their own accounts of the circumstances under which they became chiefs. Contrary to the rules of primogeniture usually followed in succession to chieftainship, neither of them was from a chiefly family. Yusuf Deng is not even from a chiefly clan. The interview was recorded in Juba on March 7, 1973, and although no people spoke besides the two chiefs and myself, with some comments from Chief Lino Aguer whom I later interviewed separately, there were a number of people present, a factor which gave the chiefs an audience for their speech-like answers.

Chief Lino Aguer is a literate Catholic convert from the Twic Dinka, and was in his early forties when I interviewed him. As a result of his basic education and religious conversion, he displays an attitude of alienation from tradition, about which he readily admits ignorance. This, however, was not simply the outcome of his education and conversion; it stemmed also from his anomalous position in traditional leadership. In fact, while I addressed him as a chief according to Dinka usage, he did not consider himself a chief, but rather a vice-president of a traditional court established in accordance with modern legislation. The interview was recorded in Juba on March 6, 1973, in the presence of a number of people including Arthur Akuien, who occasionally intervened.

Chief Albino Akot, from the Malual Dinka, was then in his early forties, a Catholic convert with a secondary education. Both his education and his political experience as a Member of Parliament had given him a wider and deeper comprehension of modern, and especially political, processes than any of the other chiefs interviewed. Nevertheless, Chief Akot remains dutiful toward the traditions of his people, which he recounts with vividness, despite the modesty of his professed ignorance. This attitude toward tradition might have been the outcome of his education, which he started in Tonj

Primary School, a government institution which was mainly
intended for sons of chiefs and officials, and was meant to
show how to base development on tradition. The fact that
Chief Akot is a son of a chief may also explain his attitude
toward tradition. This interview was conducted in Juba on
March 4, 1973, in the presence of a number of people,
including a young man called Deng Riny, also from the
Malual Dinka, who occasionally contributed.

The first Ngok interview was conducted in January 1974
in Khartoum, with Biong Mijak, Pagwot Deng, and Bulabek
Malith interviewed together. Biong was the *shiekh* (sub-chief)
of Abyor section and Pagwot the *omda* (chief) of the Bongo
section. Bulabek Malith, though from the chiefly Pajok
lineage, was not personally a chief. While Biong and Pagwot
were elders in their seventies, Bulabek, though very knowledgeable on tradition, was a younger man in his late forties
or early fifties.

The second Ngok interview was conducted in May 1974,
also in Khartoum, with Chol Adija, Loth Adija, Marieu Ajak,
and Acueng Deng interviewed together. With the exception
of Chol Adija, who had been a court member under the late
Chief Deng Majok, these informants were not chiefs but
elderly noblemen. Chol Adija was in his sixties, his half-
brother Loth in his forties, while Marieu Ajak and Acweng
Deng were men in their fifties.

Because of the peculiar political circumstances of the Ngok
Dinka, the two interviews with them were more politically
charged than any of the other interviews and, as we shall see
later, they illustrate the general policy orientation of Dinka
accounts of oral history.

The reason for selecting these contributors emanated directly from the objective of the interviews, which was not so
much to assemble a broad-based sample as it was to select a
few articulate representatives. And by this criterion the chiefs
and elders I chose were both professionally and individually

well qualified. This is not to say that the substance would necessarily have been different had the sample been numerically greater; indeed, the selected few probably say better what the larger selection would also have said, perhaps in other words.

The chiefs themselves were quite aware of the significance of what they said in terms of a representative "truth." In the following passage, Chief Yusuf Deng expressed both the importance of a broad-based source of information, and the representative capacity of the chiefs interviewed:

> A man may know something, but he will also ask about it in order to hear it repeated, and find that people say the same thing as he already knows. If he finds the same thing said over and over again, then he knows it is the truth; but if he finds that it is only the word of one man and he looks around and does not find somebody else saying the same, then he will know that this cannot be true.
>
> There are things that are made up like songs; songs are created. What one man creates is what a man makes up, but what elders say is the truth about the way a tribe runs.

I decided to focus on chiefs and prominent elders because the major themes of my investigation concerned public affairs, and the chief was traditionally the point of contact on which all information converged and, at least in theory and in conformity with his status, he was the best informed on matters of public order and cultural heritage. Even today, as many chiefs expressed it, they are viewed as "the eyes" of both the government and their people. In the words of Chief Thon Wai, the chief

> is a man who knows everything that goes on in the area. He has a microphone in his ears. By microphone, I mean the many people in his area who provide him with in-

formation. There are sub-chiefs and there are ordinary people who all come and tell him. They all come and tell the chief everything that goes on. The chief hears it and passes it on until it reaches the government. These are the words of elders.

However, while the chiefs have been used by various administrations to establish and maintain effective control over the population, the institution has usually been considered conservative and essentially inconsistent with modernity. The trend has therefore been to erode its significance, looking toward eventual abolition. This final phase has in fact been reached in the Northern Sudan. Correlative to this has been an increasing disregard of the chief and elders as the source of knowledge and wisdom, particularly as most chiefs have been illiterate. Although this attitude is now increasingly shared by the traditionals themselves, including the chiefs, they naturally find it embittering. In the words of Chol Adija:

> Educated youth have pushed us aside saying that there is nothing we know. Even if an elder talks of the important things of the country, they say, "There is nothing you know." How can there be nothing we know when we are their fathers? Did we not bear them ourselves? When we put them in school we thought they would learn new things to add to what we, their elders, would pass on to them. We hoped they would listen to our words and then add to them the new words of learning. But now it is said that there is nothing we know. This has really saddened our hearts very much.

Almost every one of those interviewed expressed appreciation in lavish terms that underscore the gap in communication between them and the educated. According to Chief Yusuf Deng: "This is a happy occasion that we have met with you. It is the first time we have met with our educated Dinka son who has been abroad." In the words of Chief Ayeny Aleu:

> Tonight I will sleep very soundly; I will sleep so soundly that even if the birds cry at night, and chickens cry, I will sleep through it all. The fact that you have called me and I have poured out of my heart everything I wanted to say, that is all I wanted.

Chief Makuei Bilkuei's words are particularly moving: "I don't drink tea and I don't drink milk. I just stay alone. When someone calls me to talk, as you called me, that is the most important thing to me. I am glad that we have now gone into the book."

Some of the older chiefs interviewed have been giant names to the Dinka for a very long time. Others are younger, but with a reputation for their dynamism, knowledge, and verbal skill. Yet others supplement the attitudes of their traditional leadership with the virtues of modern education, however limited. All in all, they are not just informants but selected individuals with a specialized perspective. We might well speak of this book as a collection of essays by men of great expertise in the fields they discuss, insofar as these fields relate to the viewpoint of the societies they lead and represent.

Of course, as I have indicated, they are also individuals with differences in age and perspective. For instance, Giirdit, representing the oldest generation, reflects a deep insight into tradition, which he recounted in fascinating detail and with an impressively calm demeanor. Men of this generation are almost oblivious to, but not naive about, modernization, which they scrutinize with the dogmatic vision of tradition. The middle group includes men not so well versed in tradition, though some individuals are exceptionally knowledgeable and articulate about it; they tend to be less interested in accounts of the past, and are almost obsessed with the present and their role in aiding development and shaping the future. This is the group now threatened and rendered insecure by the forces of modernization, and which must justify its significance by joining the wagon of change with exaggerated commitment, or otherwise perish. The younger illiterates are even more preoccupied with this than their middle-aged elders. Paradoxically, the educated chiefs are less concerned with modernization and what they can do to promote progress. They either take the matter for granted and do not feel the need for emphasis, or are quite cynical about the issue and tend to be more concerned with such personal matters as their working conditions.

On the issue of how representative the interviews are of the whole Dinka perception, there can be no doubt that the chiefs are the spokesmen of their people, especially on matters of tradition and the collective welfare of their society. When it comes to special interests within the Dinka situation, a more discriminating identification of the vested interests is called for. Such is the case with the question of how significant or relevant chieftainship is to the modern context. Originally I had analyzed the chiefs' views on this question in a separate section. I realized that they had a vested interest in this matter, but I felt that, nevertheless, it would be significant to identify this vested interest and the arguments the chiefs would use to defend their position. However, I decided to exclude the section in order to give the book a more cohesive balance, free of particularized focuses. In view of this, concern over the subjective involvement of the chiefs' perspectives should be significantly modified, for what remain are areas of general interest to the Dinka and on which all members of the society share a degree of collective biases, whatever differences there may be in matters of detail. It is perhaps worth recalling that while most of those interviewed were chiefs, some of them, notably five of the Ngok, were only elders, and at least two of the principal Southern interviewees were court presidents and not chiefs in the conventional sense. This is not to mention the ordinary persons who attended and occasionally participated. Nevertheless, there was no significant difference in the essential picture of the Dinka heritage portrayed by the chiefs and the non-chiefs, a fact which further testifies to the representational qualification of the chiefs on the general history of the Dinka.

My primary purpose in this book was to present the Dinka's own view of their heritage and contemporary situation. Such anthropologists as Godfrey Lienhardt, Edward Evans-Pritchard, and Paul Howell, whose scholarship has been based largely on Nilotic studies, are occasionally referred to. Some references are also made to the works of scholars from such disciplines as history and political science, which, though not focused on the Dinka, occasionally mention them and contribute indirectly to the promotion of better knowledge about them. In any case, I have benefited from them in formulating the theoretical or conceptual framework of the book. With respect to the literature on national integration, much of the relevant material was more directly utilized and cited in my earlier publication, *Dynamics of Identification: A Basis for National Integration in the Sudan.* In the present volume I have aimed at minimizing published references in order to preserve the originally and authentically oral character of the material.

A fundamental principle, which paradoxically gives Dinka oral history a dynamic character that makes it adaptable to current realities while also rendering it vague, ambiguous, and uncertain, is that it is transmitted by word of mouth through successive generations. Authenticity of information is largely based on the fact that the receiving generation not only listens to the transmitting generation but also has the additional advantage of proximity and observation. What they receive is revitalized through a similar process of transmission to the next generation. But logically, the more distant a generation from the source of the original information, the less reliable the information they have to pass on and the more reinforced with mythology the memory of the important aspects is in order to give them added vitality, relevancy, and effectiveness.

This fluidity of oral history is known even to the Dinka. For instance, when I asked Chief Arol Kacwol about what he had heard on creation, the origin of the Dinka, and their early migration, he said:

> The way we came is not really known to us. Those original people were created, like all people, in generations. There are generations close to our ancestors; they saw each others' ways. For instance, your generation is now watching. If anything happens, like what was happening here in the South, it will be known to you; your children too will know the day this trouble began and the day it ended.
>
> With the Dinka who do not write, each man will twist it this way and that way. Even if he reports it honestly, the truth gets lost in the middle. But a person who reads can find it all written down.

Referring to the generational transmission of history, Chief Pagwot Deng said, "That is how people grow up. . . . Each man calls his son and talks to him this way. Even if what they say is a lie, it will be what you have heard from your elders. That is how God created man." Another chief, Thon Wai, remarked after telling the stories of creation: "Those were the ancient things we heard from our fathers. They were told in conversations. They were things we heard but did not see with our own eyes. What you heard from your father and what you heard from your grandfather, you retell."

While this means that knowledge of their history is more pervasive and more broadly assimilated than is generally the case in literate societies where the sources of knowledge are available through formal institutions, it does not mean that it is equally shared nor does it mean that all are equally knowledgeable. The degree of knowledge very much depends on the dynamics of any individual situation: access to knowledgeable persons, the nature of the relationship with such persons, the interest of the recipient, and, of course, his power of retention. Bulabek Malith expressed it thus:

> Your grandfather gives you his words, the words of the land. And if you are a man who has lived among elders and you listened to them and you are a man who holds words in his heart, and you keep words in your heart well, those are the ways of learning among our people. Knowledge is what a man tells his child, a child who stays with elders. Elders will talk about the affairs of the past and a child who listens will hear them and when he one day has children, he will tell them the same things.

As a result of these dynamics, it does not always follow that the older persons are necessarily better informed than the younger. Indeed, as the reader will undoubtedly notice, some of the younger chiefs were remarkably better informed and more eloquent than their seniors.

It is quite interesting that despite reliance on memory, the long passage of time for retaining such memory, and the Dinka's own beliefs on the shortcomings of memory, they tend to recount situations with elaborate details, including interlocution, illustrating a great deal of sweeping generalization. Amidst all this complexity and uncertainty, the Dinka quite often express commitment to "the truth" and nothing but the truth. This response from Bulabek Malith to the question of what God said when man had violated his prohibition against eating the fruits of a certain tree expresses a sentiment often readily espoused by the informants. "What

God said is not clear to us. Our ancestors did not tell us that.
One does not make up stories. All we heard from the elders
was that God was angry and brought death upon men because of the woman who ate the fruit of the forbidden tree."
He might as well have talked of himself and his own elders
since a number of chiefs gave remarkable details of God's
reaction, a fact that also illustrates the diversity in the form
and degree of what is otherwise a commonly shared basic
knowledge.

As was indicated in the passage quoted from Chief Arol
Kacwol, the impact of modern education and the introduction to the world of literacy have depleted the value of
traditional knowledge to the point where the Dinka are
losing confidence in, and indeed becoming mistrustful of,
the accuracy of oral history. According to Chief Ayeny Aleu:

> About the question of where people came from, a long
> time has passed. A child with open ears listens to stories
> but they are not really true stories. They are just like
> fairy tales. Many, many years have passed . . . . It is the
> heart that tells things. It is just that our hearts are
> strong—the heart of the black man is strong—but who
> knows where we came from? We no longer know. It is a
> long time ago. We have been kept in the dark. We do not
> know much. For instance, the years I have spent in life,
> I do not know. I do not know how old I am. How can
> I know?

Chief Yusuf Deng was even reluctant to repeat any oral
history for fear of distortion.

> As for . . . ancient things, there are truly ancient things
> about our people, the Dinka. But when we tell them, we
> are likely to distort them and we will not be able to tell
> the truth. They are stories told by one generation to pass
> on to the next and from there to the next generation

and further on to the next. Such stories have been going on from the time man was created. They are told and retold until they die and get buried. The thing called head [memory] is not like a thing written down. They are not the same.

As might be expected, the educated are less knowledgeable on oral history and more suspicious of its accuracy both because they are more alienated by modern education and because of their greater faith in the written word. According to Chief Akot Awutiak: "The ancient things of our people are partly known to us, but some of them can be very difficult for us to know. This is especially the case for those of us who have not put our minds into them because of the way we have lived and the way we have been educated." Chief Lino Aguer goes beyond admitting the deficiency of his knowledge on tradition to questioning the reliability of oral history: "You know that things you hear outside are mostly things that are not recorded. But some things are recorded. The things that are recorded sound better. The things that are not recorded do not come out fully understandable."

But Lino Aguer paradoxically alleges that distortions and complications have now resulted from the recent recording of tradition in a manner that welds oral literature with other sources and presents the amalgam as an authentic Dinka version: "The way the Dinka speak of [creation] we know from what we have heard. But it is a little complicated. Some things have been written into it and it has become a little complicated. The way we heard it from our fathers is different. The way it is being said by people who have written it down is different."

While the Dinka now tend to rely on the accuracy of the written word, the traditionals also associate writing and the knowledge derived from it with a degree of secretiveness.

Commenting on his acquaintance with Arthur Akuien, himself present at the interview, Chief Ayeny Aleu remarked:

> The words of an educated man never really finish; they are all hidden there in his head and in his books. Even if you befriend an educated man to the point where you embrace one another, there is a little thing hidden in his head. Later on, when something happens that unites us, he will then tell me, "You see, this was what I thought although I did not tell you!" He will not tell me before the incidents fully occur; he will keep it all in his books and in his head.

This rather suspicious view of the secret world of the educated appears to stem from the fact that whereas traditional knowledge is open and broadly shared, modern knowledge, acquired from books as it is, is more exclusive and therefore seen as "secret."

A point which emerges clearly in the interviews is the participational standpoint which the Dinka impute to the position of the researcher. The traditional Dinka do not expect anyone to be a neutral observer. A researcher may be viewed as a person of influence by virtue of status in that society or of academic involvement. Quite apart from what he is, what he records may be seen as a way of influencing events. This is the essence of these words from Chief Ayeny Aleu.

> What you have said, you Mading, we are very pleased. Things we have told you, you will give them a purpose; you will write them down and that is a big thing.
>
> . . . If this machine of yours writes and records what a man really says, and really records well, then if what we have said is bad, it will search for our necks; if it is good, then we will say these words have saved our country. Now we have trusted you . . . we trust in you fully.

> Whatever you think we have missed, whatever you think
> we should have said that we missed, let it be said that we
> are the people who said it.

Referring to an alternative suggestion I had made for government policy toward the Ngok Dinka, Marieu Ajak observed,
"What you are doing is correct. Write it down; write it down;
it is the truth." After listing a number of things he felt were
urgently needed, Acueng Deng said, "Those are the things I
wanted to tell you . . . you will find them in the machine.
Write them down." Not infrequently, I was asked to record
the points made in their order of priority. "Of all things,"
said Chief Ayeny Aleu,

> put the question of water first; write it down first, let
> water come so that we can drink. If a man has had water
> to drink, so that he is not thirsty, he can fight in a feud.
> Let us get water first. Other things are machinery for
> cultivating the fields and medicine for the cure of peo-
> ple and for the cure of cattle.

This policy orientation means that the researcher will be
given information according to how best the participant-
informant believes he can influence the outcome in his—the
informant's—own interest as an individual, a member of a
family line, or an advocate of one system or another.

For me, the situation was made more involved and complex
by both my family standing in Dinka society as the son of
a paramount chief and my own public position. This was a
significant consideration behind the frankness with which I
was given information and therefore the insight I acquired
through the interviews. My standpoint as an objective collec-
tor of information was often ignored or subordinated to my
public responsibility as a leader, and demands were made on
me which were based on the fundamental assumption of
my involvement. This statement from Chief Yusuf Deng is

typical of the attitude of most chiefs: "We will listen to you
tell us about the affairs of running the country." Chief
Ayeny Aleu was even more categorical in his reversal of my
position.

> What I want to say to you now is that it is not for us to
> tell you if our country is now in order and things are
> going well, if this will happen or we should do this or do
> that! That is not so. It is you who will tell us, "If we put
> this right, we will acquire strength. If we put this right,
> we will have a shelter from the rain. If we do things this
> and that way, this is how we shall be strong. This is how
> we should proceed." That part we are leaving to you in
> our conversation. It will be for you to talk to us and we
> will listen and then talk to you. If there is something in
> what you say that doesn't appeal to me, I will turn to
> you and say, "Son, why have you put it this and that
> way? Why is it that things are this and that way?" And
> if it is a good word you tell us, we will follow you. And
> I will go and tell the people all over Dinkaland. In my
> part of Dinkaland I will tell them that in our conversation
> in Juba, what I have been told is this and that; that this
> is the way we should proceed in our country. We will
> begin to push the boundaries of our fields; we will push
> them on and on and on. But as to the words of how we
> should run our country, we must speak our minds; there
> is nothing to hide; we should speak freely.

In the words of Chief Arol Kacwol, "If there is something
which is now harming the country and you hear of it later
instead of now, you will say, 'Did I not talk to these people?
Why did they not mention it it me?' . . . So, what I am saying I want you to hear it well."

Chief Stephen Thongkol Anyijong, like Chief Ayeny Aleu,
saw in our interview both a general and a particular purpose:
"If a single man comes, like Mading who has now come, we

will give him our complaints. And if he talks to those big leaders, he can tell them, 'The chiefs feel this way; what can you do for them?' Then we hope they can think about our problems. As Chief Arol said to you, we chiefs work for the people behind you."

The Ngok informants in particular were so blatant about their policy orientation that sometimes it was hard to adhere to the themes I had postulated for my interviews. The position was presented by Bulabek Malith in the following words:

> You know, Mading, as we talk to you today, our hearts will cool down because you have been found. The pains of the past will cool down because, if people have talked to you, then people hope that you can do something. You are a man who is educated and who has been made a leader. People may respect you. We cannot be sure, but that is why we tell you the thoughts of our tribe and the things that have been disturbing us in this country.

Chief Biong Mijak was indeed vexed by my determination to follow the research line rather than address myself to the issues that were of concern to the tribe.

> What we should also talk about are the things of today. That is why you said yesterday that we should come today at five o'clock. Our words have been going around, but this is something we should have talked about earlier. We are happy that you have come. Today we are absent from home. If they hear that the chiefs have met Mading, the politicians (opportunists) may not realize it, but our people will say, "We will hear a good word coming back with them."

Because of participational dynamics and policy considerations, the manner in which the Dinka give information, especially with respect to claims of ancestral roles in the history of the Dinka, is not free from sensitivities, tensions,

and conflicts, particularly when the situation involves competing descent groups, such as chiefly families. This was strikingly revealed by Giirdit's demeanor in our interview. Having
made no reference to the myths of chieftainship and their
ancestral role in it, I asked him to tell me the myth of Ayuel
Longar which he, Giirdit, had recounted to Lienhardt and
according to which Giirdit's ancestor, Agothyithiik, saved the
Dinka from the malevolence of Ayuel Longar, who was
killing people by spearing them as they tried to cross the
river. Agothyithiik subdued him and thus permitted the
people to cross. Longar then gave Agothyithiik and his asso-
ciates divine power and they became the founding fathers of
chiefly lineages.

The Ngok Dinka of Kordofan, however, have a number of
myths that attribute the original paramount leadership of
the Dinka to the Pajok, the family which leads the Ngok.
The origin of their leadership is dated back to the time of
creation. Athurkok, the praise-name of Jok, who founded the
clan, means "the one who broke through" and symbolizes
his leadership from "the Byre of Creation." Jok is said to
have defeated the competitor, Longar, in a series of confron-
tations which resulted in Longar ultimately surrendering any
claims to spiritual leadership. In his version to Lienhardt,
Giirdit had referred to Jok as one of the descendants of his
main lineage whose descendants ultimately seem to pre-
dominate: "Jok became big and took the land" and "Mathi-
ang Dit [a praise-name for some unnamed person], the son
of Jok, became important and seized the country." Lienhardt
notes that "The sub-tribes in which the Pajok main lineage
has primacy are large and flourishing." It is apparent from all
this that Giirdit and I represented families with competing
leadership claims. Therefore, when I raised the issue of Ayuel
Longar's myth, Giirdit suddenly found himself confronted
with the predicament of how best to gear his version toward
harmonizing our competing claims. It was fascinating to see

such an articulate elder suddenly become almost incoherent
as he searched for the appropriate response.

> Chieftainship . . . I don't know whether ours was differ-
> ent from yours and other people's—but this is how
> chieftainship started. It started with people a long time
> ago. Hi [Yes] . . . It started . . . It started . . . Yes . . . I
> don't know whether it started with Longar. It is with
> Longar that it started. He made himself a deceiver of
> people. And when the people came to the river, he said
> nobody was to cross, nobody was to dive across to the
> other side. And if anybody did, he was to face the spirit
> of the river. He killed many people that way. It is said
> that a person called . . . What is his name? . . . called
> Awer Awuciu and a man called Agothyithiik and an-
> other man called Akuien were the people who held him.

In his version to Lienhardt, Giirdit had named his ancestor
Agothyithiik first and then "Awuciu" as his only helper. Dr.
Lienhardt attributed this to the fact that there were representatives of Awuciu's small lineage near Giirdit's mother's
home. It is interesting that in our interview Giirdit added the
name of Akuien as another helper of his ancestor, and then
proceeded to wonder whether my family did not descend
from Akuien. When I further asked which way the three
original leaders led the Dinka in their migration, Giirdit was
still eager to involve my ancestral leadership by saying,
"Well, they have produced the Ngok like you," still asserting
"Your ancestor is Akuien."

As I found it necessary to be at least cautiously supportive
in the circumstances, I said, "It's like what I heard among
the Ngok in my clan—that our clan is so large and dispersed
that wherever you go you find a different name for it." At
this point, Giirdit's eldest son, Mou, came to our rescue by
claiming that we were in fact one clan with them. "Well,
actually," he said, "the name of the clan Paghol [their clan]

includes Pajok. It has also the Pakuien and the Pajong."
His father then continued the point by including more
names under the one umbrella of his ancestral tree. I was of
course aware of Giirdit's earlier version to Lienhardt and
the part that made Jok a member of his lineage. My attention
had also been drawn to a part of our genealogy which referred to the founder of our clan as Jok Athurkok, the son
of "Mother of Angau," a name which brought to mind
"Anau" in Giirdit's version to Lienhardt. With this background
information I was quite prepared to believe in some distant
relationship and therefore welcomed the compromise.

When I recounted to Ngok elders what had transpired between Giirdit and myself, they categorically dismissed Giirdit's claim about his family's share in original chieftainship,
maintaining that there was no equal to Jok. Chol Adija
indiscreetly asserted with reference to Giirdit's claim, "That
is a lie." When I asked Chief Arol Kacwol about the myths
of original leadership, and told him of my conversation with
Giirdit about Longar, he remarked diplomatically: "How it
happened we have not been able to know fully, we the later
generations. But man is such that with stories like that of
Longar, each person has his view. As you have just said,
Giirdit has his view of what happened."

This tendency of the Dinka to assume a participational interest or role for the researcher and to gear accounts of their
history in favor of their lineages is an aspect of the wider
tendency to give a purpose to history by giving it functional
objectives. As I indicated earlier, this purpose-orientation of
history was strikingly illustrated by the accounts of the Ngok
Dinka interviews which were conducted under two different
circumstances and as a result reflect almost opposite sentiments. When I conducted the first set of interviews, the
South-North civil war had ended and violence had ceased, but
the Ngok had not been included in the newly established
autonomy, nor in the programs of relief, resettlement, and

rehabilitation, and therefore saw little if any reason for rejoicing. Their situation remained politically charged, explo-
sive, and substantially unchanged.

As is apparent, the first set of Ngok interviewees was so affected by the misery they were in and the bitterness they felt
against the North that a feeling of alienation and hostility
pervades their view of history from creation to speculations
on the future. However unrelated to the issue of North and
South my questions were, their answers always led back to
the profound dichotomy they felt existed and had always
existed between them and the Arabs.

Chief Biong Mijak typified the extremism that was their
viewpoint:

> Our ancestors, when they came, had nothing to do with
> the Arabs. Even when they met they fought, killing one
> another. The Arabs wanted slaves and the Dinka refused
> to accept that. . . . This black world belonged to the
> Dinka from the beginning. . . . Our ancestors came from
> the cattle-byre quite distinct. We are not the same people
> as the Arabs.

To the question of whether integration between the South
and the North was possible in the long run, Bulabek Malith
spoke of Arab slave raids against the Dinka and concluded:

> This behavior [of the Arabs] we encountered a long, long
> time ago. And we have long observed it. If they were a
> people who could abandon their vile manners, they
> would have abandoned them a long time ago. But these
> are a people whom God created in their own way. From
> the time of Creation, they liked things like slavery; they
> love slavery. Even if people become really equal and the
> South gets educated and has full freedom, the way elders
> like us see it in their hearts, it seems that they will one
> day separate. The Northerner is a person you cannot say
> will one day mix with the Southerner to the point where

the blood of the Southerner and the blood of the Arab will become one.

When I conducted the second set of Ngok interviews, the situation had begun to change. Despite the short lapse in time, significant political steps had been taken to implement a form of autonomy and develop the area, and some of the measures that had been under way were becoming associated with the new policy. Ten well-selected local government administrators had been posted to Abyei where there had been none, and a Ngok had been appointed Province Deputy Commissioner to head the local administration. A number of Ngok Dinka policemen, school teachers, and other officials had also been transferred to Abyei. Several tractors had been received to mechanize agriculture. A modern medical center had been established. A junior secondary school had been opened. And a number of other reforms had been introduced as initial steps in what was envisaged to be a major development program in the area.

As might be expected, the attitude of those interviewed was remarkably positive. In sharp contrast with the earlier emphasis on differences and hostilities, the emphasis had shifted to factors that united. Chol Adija reflected the changed attitude when he remarked:

> This country of ours was one. There was no South and there was no North. It was one single country. And the Great Arob Biong [of the Ngok] was the one on top of the land. When a small fight broke out between the North and the South, he protected the South. . . . The Arabs, it is me, the Ngok, whom they know; the Twic, it is me, the Ngok, whom they know. As Chief Deng said, "I am the thread of the center"; it is true, we are the thread between the South and the North. The Ngok links them both, the North and the South. The North is his and the South is his. They meet there at Abyei; Abyei is a place for everybody.

On the question of prospects for integration, which the Dinka quickly associate with intermarriage, the trend had also changed. The words of Marieu Ajak were quite reflective of the general attitude.

> As I see it, in the future of our world I think we shall marry Arab girls and I believe the Arabs will marry our girls. The country wants to mix and it is already beginning to mix. We shall be one. . . . Our girls used to refuse Arabs in the past. Today, they accept them. . . . I believe our country has become one and, as I see it, we shall intermarry in the future.

Only Chol Adija, an older man, maintained a hard conservative line: "What kind of marriages do you say exist now? Marriages with prostitutes? Have you seen any decent girl, a daughter of a gentleman, marrying an Arab?" But there was a uniform disagreement with him: his own brother, Loth, said almost condescendingly: "Chol, can't you see that there is mixing right now? Son of my father, they will marry."

The Dinka assumption of the participational standpoint of any researcher, and their own policy orientation in the manner and content of their information, are challenges to objectivity about which a participant-observer must be especially concerned, but also have the advantage of giving deep insights into the policy thinking of the informants. Because of my involvement as a participant-observer, the form and possibly the nature of the information I was given might have been affected, perhaps both negatively and positively, but I daresay my standpoint opened avenues of mutual confidence and structural insights which are usually not available in standard research by the more "detached" outside observers. The point was aptly made by Chief Ayeny Aleu when he insisted on knowing my standpoint before talking freely.

> I am very pleased that you have called me. I praise you very much for this. . . . But before I talk any further, would you tell me, are you talking to me as a Dinka? I

ask you because our country is still in the hands of the Northerners and, as you know, our country has remained far behind the North. Today, as you talk to me, are you after the words of your own people, the people of your father, Deng, and of your grandfather, Kwol, or do you want these words from us as the representative of the law? That is the first thing I must ask about before I talk any further. I must understand; if you are a Northerner, then frankly, some words will remain unspoken.

For the same reason that confidence and group solidarity were prerequisite, if mostly assumed, conditions for the frankness with which information was given, I had to grapple with the problem of what to publish and in what form. That the material was to be published was made clear in my introductory remarks before every interview. Not only was that welcome to the people interviewed, it usually acted as an incentive, for it assured them of the importance I attached to the interviews and the wide audience that publication would guarantee them. Indeed, I was sometimes expressly urged to give them the widest possible publicity. Chief Ayeny Aleu, in addition to asking me to "put them in the newspapers," said:

> Even if we have said something that can kill us, please write it down as we said it. Let us die; if we die and the South remains united and free, then it is well; let it be said that we are the people who said these things and that we should die for them. We would welcome that.

Chief Stephen Thongkol, responding to my quest for frankness, said:

> I must tell you that I can never fear. There is nothing that I fear at all. Even to the Arabs themselves I would say what I want to say now. Even if they were here now, I would not hide anything. I am a man who doesn't fear

death. If I die, then I have children. If there is a Southerner with a light heart, I will talk to him frankly and I will leave my children behind. I don't fear anything.

These remarks show that while the chiefs were made aware that the objective was to publish the material and they welcomed that prospect, they were also aware of possible dangers. Indeed, Akuien and I felt it necessary at the end to say something reassuring to them. Akuien made the statement.

Chief Mading asked me to tell you something. You said that you have given your names away and that whatever goes wrong, you are willing to sacrifice yourselves for whatever you might have said. I thought I should tell you that what Mading is doing, he knows it will not put you in trouble. It cannot put you in trouble. What you have said we want to put into books to be read by our children and by the children of our children.

Of course, I also assured each one of them that I would be selective in what to publish. What was too confidential or inappropriate to publish, I would withhold and guard in confidence. This has not, however, been easy to do, for such selection is of necessity subjective and does impose on the material the danger of distorting the total balance that the narrator might have envisaged. As a result, I have been most sparing in my omissions. It is therefore appropriate that I should appeal to my readers to consider it my full responsibility, should things have been included which in their judgment should not have been published.

2. The Origin of Things

Creation

To the Dinka, the origination of things in the world and the universe implies creation as the work of God, but the other fundamental association the Dinka make with God is of the negation of creation by destruction; together these concepts explain the worldly focus of Dinka religion and its emphasis on the moral content or lack of it as the source of indulgences or deprivations. In both the myths of creation and the moral content of their religion, Dinka mythology and philosophy bear surprisingly close kinship with the universalizing scriptures of the Middle East: Judaism, Christianity, and Islam. On the face of it, one is tempted to find an easy explanation in the close contact the Dinka have recently had with missionaries. Closer examination, however, suggests that the roots must be deeper. In the following pages, I shall give a brief account of the nature of Dinka religion, their concept of God, their myths of creation, and the possible explanation of the similarities between these myths and those of the Holy Books.

Much has been written about Nilotic religions which shows that they largely aim at the well-being of man in a living society rather than at individual survival after death. They do have a notion of continued physical existence in the underground world of the dead and a spiritual linkage of that world with that of the living and the powers above, but their concepts in this respect are rather nebulous and, despite the similarities in other respects, tend to differ from the Heaven and Hell concepts popularly associated with Christianity and Islam. The focus of their concept of immortality is in this world, through procreation and agnatic lineage continuation, which lead to ancestral veneration, almost culminating in worship. In the words of British anthropologist Godfrey Lienhardt, "Dinka fear to die without male issue, in whom the survival of their names—the only kind of immortality they know—will be assured."[1]

This fear was indirectly or conversely indicated by a number of chiefs who expressed willingness to die in self-sacrifice for the country. Chief Ayeny Aleu said, "Let us die as long as we leave our children behind to continue our names." Chief Stephen Thongkol Anyijong remarked, "I am a man who does not fear death. If I die, then I have children." As Chief Thon Wai indicated, children are the greatest treasure for the Dinka and it is with reference to them that the labors of life are explained.

> When a man works, he does not work for his own sake; he works for a child he has created. It is for children in the neighborhood that a man works. It is for the children of the South that a Southerner must work. You do not work for your own sake; you work for the children of the country. You do for them things they will grow up and find.

As might be expected, it is considered desirable for a man to have as many children as he can. While spacing children is practiced through customary rituals of sexual avoidance which are explained in terms of health or aesthetic considerations, birth control by married couples is unknown. By extension, this logic favors the increase of population in the wider structural contexts, and, provided the increase is not unnaturally excessive, any slowing of population growth is left to God and the balances of nature. It is this last point

1. Godfrey Lienhardt, *Divinity and Experience* (Oxford, Clarendon Press, 1961), p. 26.

Chief Biong Mijak made when, referring to the myths of the forbidden tree and the potsherd that the woman threw into the river, causing God to afflict the hitherto immortal man with death, he said, "If the woman had not done that, people would have been too many." According to a myth related by Father Nebel, after the first man and woman had borne a child, God told them, "Your child will die, but after only fifteen days he will return." The man, here known as Garang, disagreed and said, "If people return again, they will be too numerous. Where will they build their homes? There will not be enough land."[2]

Despite this realistic mythical approach to the potential problem of excessive population, procreation remains a fundamental Dinka value and modality. According to the account of Chief Pagwot Deng, that was the reason for the creation of the woman: "God almost decided not to create the woman. But the man said, 'How will people multiply? Will people not stop with this one number? Even if people do not die, even if people live without death, should people not increase?'" Indeed, although his words are rather contradictory and somewhat confused, Pagwot seems to suggest some connection between the subsequent wrong of the woman in eating the forbidden fruit and God's initial reluctance to create her. Wanting the woman to be created and eating the forbidden fruit are synonymously presented as engineered by the snake and are associated with the need for procreation.

> The story of the tree is the story of the woman. . . . The woman was deceived by a snake who said, "How can you go without eating this fruit? How can you survive without a woman? It is the woman who will bear children. . . . How can people be created without a woman?" So they were created with the woman.

2. Ibid., p. 36.

Dinka criteria for sharing spiritual and material values are largely determined by the hierarchies implicit in their agnatic procreational concept, with men having priority over women, the older over the younger, the dead over the living, and the spirits over the humans.

Despite its group interests, lineage continuation implies a diversity and maybe conflict of interests, especially as between male contemporaries or generations which must compete, or succeed one another, in the collective and yet individual search for immortality. Lienhardt observed:

> The Dinka positively value the unity of their tribes, and of their descent groups, while also valuing that autonomy of their component segments which can lead to fragmentations. The basis of this occasional contradiction of values lies in each Dinka ambition. . . . A man . . . wishes to belong to a large descent group, because the greater the numbers of his agnatic kin who have still not formally segmented with separate agnatic groups, the wider the range of people from whom he can hope for help . . . in quarrels either within the tribe or outside it. On the other hand, each man wants to found his own descent group, a formal segment of the sub-clan which will for long be remembered by his name, and wants to withdraw from his more distant agnatic kin in order not to be required to help. . . . These values of personal autonomy and of cooperation, of the inclusiveness and unity of any wider political or genealogical segments and the exclusiveness and autonomy of its several subsegments are from time to time in conflict.[3]

The Dinka are so aware of this generational tension that a prudent father deliberately prepares his sons for a timely retirement and a harmonious handing over of family re-

3. Godfrey Lienhardt, "Western Dinka," in *Tribes Without Rulers*, ed. John Middleton and David Tait (London, Routledge & Paul, 1958), pp. 117–18.

sponsibility to the next generation. For the same reason the Dinka consciously develop in their children, particularly males, a combination of filial piety with self-reliance and self-assertiveness, even as against the father, whenever the rights of the child are unduly infringed upon. As one Dinka put it, "A child who does not object to his father's ill-treatment of him is not in his father's image." Chief Arol Kacwol expressed the concept of procreational immortality, generational succession, and its psychological implications in the following words:

> It is God who changes the world by giving successive generations their turns. For instance, our ancestors, who have now disappeared, by the way their world began and the way they lived, they held the horns of their life. Then God changed things; things changed until they reached us; and they will continue to change. When God comes to change your world, it will be through you and your wife. You will sleep together and bear a child. When that happens, you should know that God has passed to your children borne by your wife the things with which you lived your life. For instance, your father, Deng Majok, if he had lived without a child until his death, his would have been the kind of life that continues only as a tale. But if he bore a big son like you who can be spoken of—"This is Mading, son of Deng"— then, even if a person has never met your father and he hears that you are the son of Deng in the same way he had heard of your father, he will meet through you your father whom he never met.

Implicit in procreational immortality is the extension of familial concepts into the spiritual world, thus leading to the designation of deities in ancestral terms as "grand-fathers," and the identification of particular deities with particular families. Even God, whom the Dinka believe to be all-embracing, is identified in such descent terms as "God of my Grandfather," "God of my Father," "God, my Grandfather," or "God, my Father."

Despite claims of familial identification with God, the Dinka, as Lienhardt noted, "assert with a uniformity which makes the assertion almost a dogma that 'God is One.' They cannot conceive of God as a plurality and, did they know what it meant, would deeply resent being described as polytheistic."[4] Nonetheless, the Dinka believe in a hierarchy of deities, some good and some bad; some "related" to particular clans and some "free" to be acquired or to "fall" on individuals of their own choice; some moralistic in their judgment of human beings and some capricious; some protective and some destructive. The powers of these spirits are sometimes identified with the Over-All God and each of these spirits is sometimes designated as "God."

In his accounts of the myths of creation, Chief Makuei Bilkuei, for instance, equates Deng with God although Deng is a spirit which, though presumably next to God in importance, is also subordinate to the One All-Embracing God. According to Chief Makuei, "Deng of the sky took mud and created the first person; he made him a man." The man later complained, "You Deng of the sky, you have created me badly. How can I stay all alone and eat alone without somebody to speak to me?" In the middle of the night, "God" came and took his rib and made the woman from it. On the myth of the tower with which man tried to reach God, Makuei also said, "His plan was to reach Deng of the sky. He wanted to reach God above there." Thus Deng is used interchangeably with God.

It is this complexity of multiplicity in unity that blurs the monotheistic nature of Dinka religion, which is otherwise unquestionable. The One God is essentially virtuous even though he may be angered by the wrongful deeds of

4. Lienhardt, *Divinity and Experience*, p. 156.

man and may himself impose a punishment or refrain from
protecting man from the malevolence of evil spirits.

The Dinka do not speculate on whether there is God or
not, for, to them, evidence of his existence is abundant in the
very being of man, the earth, and the universe, with all
their contents, animate and inanimate. To the more recent
doubts of sophisticated skeptics, a traditional rhetorical
question is "Who created you?" In the words of Chief Arol
Kacwol: "It is God who holds the country with his own
power. He creates the people and keeps them as he keeps
the trees which grow in the forest. All these are the works
of God: he has created the human beings who speak; he has
created some to become elders; others to be only children;
and yet others to be women."

The Dinka explain man's ignorance of God's precise where-
abouts, the concrete facts of how he originally created man
and the universe, and the suffering and eventual death that
man now undergoes by a number of myths which they
recount with a degree of consistency and uniformity. In all
these myths, God is conceived as having been in close contact
with man in this world. Suffering and death did not exist or,
according to some versions, when people died they were
recreated. On the whole, life was then perfect. According to
various versions, the connection with God was severed owing
to the fault of the human being or some earthly creature,
thus forcing God to withdraw, willing that the world be
immersed in suffering, misery, and death.

Perhaps the most universal myth, which the Dinka tell in
detail, is that of the sacred tree which God forbade the first
man and woman to eat. Under the temptation of the snake,
the woman succumbed and broke her promise to God. Her
husband later followed suit in solidarity with his wife. All
three got their respective punishments.

According to Chief Makuei Bilkuei, man was first created,
given food every morning, and told, "This tree you must not

eat." Then he asked for a companion and the woman was created from his rib.

And when the big snake called Biar [Brown Snake] saw that the man had gone for a walk, he met the woman and said, "If you eat this tree, God will give you a very good thing."

She said, "But God himself said that we should not eat this tree!"

The snake said, "Eat it while the man is away. This tree will do for you great things."

She looked at it, then she tasted it. As soon as she had a bite of that fruit, she saw God. Then she sat with her head bent down.

When the man came, he said, "My wife, why are you bending your head down?"

She said, "The snake came and made me eat the tree."

The man cried and said, "We had better die together. If you have eaten it, what shall I do? We had better go together."

God came at night and said, "Adam, did you eat this tree?"

Adam said, "Yes."

"Who began it?" God asked.

"The snake," said Adam.

And God said, "I have something to tell you. From today, I'll make your life unpleasant."

He called the woman and he called the snake and he said, "Did you plan all this?"

The snake said, "Yes."

God said, "Well, from today, you will only crawl; you will not walk again."

And God gave the man the hoe and said, "This is your hoe. If you do not cut trees and cultivate and sweat, you will not eat. And you woman, you will suffer great pain when you bear children. The snake will bite your children and bearing children will kill you."

In the account of Chief Thon Wai, which is equally vivid, there were a number of trees, perhaps of the same kind.

All mankind had one mother. But man was created first. . . . That's what we heard from the ancient past. What is called woman was a rib of the man. When the man was alone on this earth, he sat mourning for days. And when he was so sad and he cried, "Why must I be so lonely without someone to help me?" God pulled his rib out of him and made the woman. And God said one thing: "Tomorrow, when it dawns, these trees, which I have planted near the cattle-byre next to the garden in which durra is cultivated, there is not a single tree you are to touch. These trees are bad; don't eat them. But these other trees are good; you may eat them."

And when the man went away on an errand one creature called Lualdit [the Great Brown Snake] came. He approached the woman and said, "You, how can you leave such a delicious fruit? Here it is, eat it."

When she saw it she said, "This food God forbade us. We can't eat it. It's a bad fruit."

But he said, "It is a good fruit."

So the woman succumbed. Hers was a small heart of a woman which easily changes. So she tasted it, and as soon as she tasted it, it turned into a bad thing. So the woman sat mourning and crying. She just sat crying. And when the man returned he said to her, "Why do you sit like that?"

She said, "The person spoke to me!"

"What person?"

"The person called Snake."

"What did he tell you?"

"He said to me, "Eat that fruit."

"The tree that God had refused? How could you eat it? You've done a terrible thing. But never mind, it's good, nothing is altogether bad. What can we do? Let me taste it too. Since you've tasted it, how can I not taste it too? It's better that we die together."

So they went together. They found themselves a tree under which to hide. But God heard everything. That's how God came and said, "You, there is nothing I will say any more. Each person must survive through his own strength. What he works for is what he will eat. Each man will eat the sweat that comes out of his body. He will earn his food by his own strength. And everything he will bring by his own strength. And you will return into this earth from which I created you man and took your rib and made the woman who has now turned against me by doing a bad thing. Both of you will now suffer. The woman will bear children in pain and you both will meet with suffering and death."

The account of Loth Adija adds other dimensions.

People were created in the way I said earlier. And the fruits had ripened on the trees. God said, "There is nothing for you to eat." So he gave them trees from which to find food. But there was one tree about which he said to them, "Do not touch this one tree; do not eat it; do not touch it." People say that the tree does not exist in this country.

This big snake, which now bites people, used to have legs. He came and found the people hungry. He said to the woman, "What about this tree? This tree which is so ripe in front of your home?"

The woman said, "God has forbidden; he says we should not eat it; if we eat it, he will kill us."

The snake had feet and used to walk in the same way

the dog and other animals walk. He said to the woman, "Eat the tree."

So she went and pulled the fruit from the tree and ate it. When the man came he said, "Why did you do this?"

She said, "The snake said that what God had said is a lie; it is because the tree is delicious that he keeps it from us."

When God came he said, "So you have truly taken the fruit of this tree and eaten it."

They said, "Yes." . . . The man too had eaten the fruit.

God then said, "If you have eaten this tree, then you will never see it again. This has been your last chance to eat it. I will take it away. It will never grow on this soil of yours and it will never grow anywhere on this earth. And who made you eat it?"

They said, "It was the Snake!"

God said to the Snake, "So it was you, Snake, who made them eat the tree?"

"Yes," said the Snake.

He then said, "In that case, you will never have legs on you again. You will only crawl on your belly. Even a person who could not have been able to kill you when you had legs will now be able to kill you as you crawl on your belly. You will no longer have legs with which to run like all the other creatures."

Legs then disappeared from the snake. The tree also disappeared from the land.

Then God stopped making all the things he had promised to create and give to man. Even a thing called "What," which he had said he would give to man, he kept from man.

According to Marieu Ajak eating the forbidden fruit was synonymous with loving the woman more than God.

God said to man, "You have now spoiled your good

things by eating the tree. You were going to eat good things without any sweat on your body. But if you have so loved the woman, then you will do everything with sweat on your body. You will cut down trees and that will be your food. Your body will pour with sweat, but you will never see 'What' again. You will toil on the land for your food. You will look for everything with your own strength. You have played with the food you would have eaten without toil."

Another myth by which the suffering of man is popularly explained is that of the small blue bird called Atacgong which cut the rope that linked God to man. This myth is told by Loth Adija as though it were separate from the myth of the forbidden tree but the role of the woman is also reflected and associated with procreation or childbirth. "It is said that Atacgong had newly given birth. . . . Polished grain was spread to dry in the open air. Then came the hunger of a woman who has newly delivered. So she went to eat the grain." Here Marieu Ajak interjected a sentence which illustrates the shared knowledge of this myth: "It [the grain] was spread out in a tray of woven straws." Loth continued:

Yes, it was spread out in a tray of woven straws. She was sent away from the grain. So she went and lay down in the place where she had newly delivered. It is said that she starved to death lying there. Her husband jumped up and flew away in anger. God was so near that whenever any problem was too big for a person, he could find God near to help him. If anything threatened man with death, he could run and climb up the rope to get help from God. But the husband of Atacgong went and cut the rope. He immediately severed the earth from God. It was delivery which did it. He cut the rope and brought hatred.

Yet another myth by which the Dinka explain death is that

of the woman who threw a potsherd into the river. The myth was recounted here by Loth Adija with introductory remarks by his brother, Chol, who described her action as part of the irrational behavior of women. Loth however explained her conduct differently and movingly.

The woman was blind. And the river was teeming with fish. Plenty of fish were being caught. And then, as the people were catching fish, she held to a stick held by her small granddaughter who led her to the riverside. As people were carrying their fish away, she begged, "O people, I am a blind woman without a child; give me from your catch of fish."

The man who was ahead of everybody took a fish and threw it down in front of her; one fish.

When the next person came, she said, "Please give me fish. I am a blind woman without someone to fish for me."

He picked up the same fish and threw it down in front of her. That was seen by all those who followed. Each man came and took that same fish and threw it down. All those who were fishing passed by. And it was the same fish the first man had given which each person took and threw down in front of her.

When they had all passed, she said, "Daughter of my daughter, what will all this fish be carried in?"

The child said, "O grandmother, it is that single fish which the first man threw down."

"Now?" she said.

"Yes," said the child.

She went and felt the fish and then continued to feel all around her. She thought the child was joking. She looked and looked and when she found that it was truly that one fish, she said, "Very well!"

Then she said to God, "God, you have created blindness so that a person gets blind."

People used to become blind in old age. And when you were completely old, so that your days were finished, you were remolded and recreated to become young again. The blind woman then called for the thing called death. She took a segment of gourd. She prayed over it and threw it into the water. The sherd floated on the river; it did not sink. She asked, "What happened to it?"

They said, "It has surfaced and is floating on the water."

She said, "Bring it back."

Then she took a potsherd and again prayed. After she threw it into the water, she asked, "What happened to it?"

They said, "It has sunk."

Then she said, "God, as you brought blindness, you will also bring death in the way the potsherd has gone. A person will die and never return. It is returning from death which has spoiled the people so much."

That's it. When a person died the following morning, he was buried and people thought he would return. But he disappeared forever. That is how people began to die and never return.

According to the foregoing myths, labor and suffering came from the forbidden tree and the broken rope while death came from the potsherd that the woman threw into the water. But this attempt at rationalizing and harmonizing the myths is irrelevant to the Dinka for whom the myths symbolize and explain God's severance from man and the consequent hardships of that separation.

A recurrent theme of Dinka religious thought and practice is to implore God to restore the erstwhile unity and goodness, the human need for which becomes acute when man suffers the misfortunes of sickness and death. This in itself shows that although separated from man and despite human suffering and death, God is not entirely removed from man's cognizance. Man sees evidence of him in all the unexplained wonders of life, nature, and the universe.

God's proximity and continued help to man, especially in his procreative pursuits, is lucidly expressed by Chief Ayeny Aleu in this passage.

Where God created people, I don't really know. It is very difficult to imagine in one's mind. But he did create people. And he did not leave us; the creator did not leave us. Why? There is one thing which makes me believe that the thing that created us was good and is near. For instance, your mother was married and what she did with your father was a game; they were playing a game of pleasure. And that game has now become Mading.

So, you see, can we really say that the creator has gone away? He is here and he is good. Here is Mading, and it all began with a game between your father and your mother, between Deng Kwol and your mother. Here you have emerged as Mading and you have satisfied all of us. So, you see why we are happy?

To the Dinka, procreation is more than a consequence of sex, for heredity, on which the Dinka place great importance, is envisioned as an outcome of a whole sequence of socio-biological factors, including parental relations, environmental conditions, and spiritual considerations. To quote again from Chief Ayeny Aleu:

A father gives his heart to his son if there is happiness between him and his wife. Heredity is a matter of happiness. When a man enters his mother's womb through his father's sperm [literally, urine of birth], it is the happiness of his father and his mother which gives him his father's good blood. The father passes on to the son his best qualities if he is happy at the moment of his sleeping with the mother. If your father had quarreled with your mother, you would not have entered your mother's womb with the qualities you now have. I, for instance, if my wife tells me a bad thing and I blindly go into bed with her, the child I will beget will never get my qualities. And as you sit here now, it is because of the good food your mother cooked for your father and the good words they said to one another that you came out just like your father. That is why Deng Kwol begot you so straight with his qualities.

Nevertheless, the Dinka consider procreation to be in effect a work of God through the instrumentality of man and woman. As God reflects the realities of this largely unexplained and, to the Dinka, unexplainable world, he symbolizes both fortune and mishap, and while the consequences of virtuous conduct are presumably good, afflictions by God are never ruled out in any matter, including procreation. Indeed, there is abundant evidence in Dinka experience to suggest that God not only may, but often does, display a nature which is both harsh and gentle, both cruel and kind.

Chief Arol Kacwol expressed the point in these spiritually moving words: "No man is the creator of good, son of Deng Majok; it is God who creates goodness and it is he who causes it to turn bad. When trouble comes, as it did between us and the Northerners, it all returns to God. And if things again go back to their original goodness, it is God who holds their feet and brings them back to the ground."

Thus, the Dinka notion of God and religion is intimately associated with Dinka experience, conceptually originating in creation and embracing all phases of human existence within the framework of cosmic totality. The multiplicity and unity of the divine order itself represents the unity and diversity embodied in this cosmic totality. Unification and diversification of experience extend to the whole of man and his environment.

Chief Thon Wai indicated the interdependencies of the cosmic whole when he appraised President Nimeri's achievement in ending the civil war between the South and the North.

> He has brought people together. Even the goat and the sheep and the fish in the river have seen what Jaafar Nimeri has done. What he has done has brought peace to the dog, to the goat, to the sheep, and even to the fish in the river. Nimeri's work has brought life to all these creatures. This word is a word of truth and life.

And in another context Chief Thon, referring to the universality of the human worth, said, "Even the creatures we call lions are humans. Those creatures we say eat people were born as part of this living world." Chief Makuei Bilkuei expressed a similar view when he advocated an all-embracing concept of national unity.

> Our blood, the blood of the black skin, was one. It is the government which has taken harmony away, because black skin was one with our hyenas, with our leopards, with our elephants, with our buffaloes; we were all one skin. We are one people. . . . We should all combine—the people, the animals, the birds that fly—we are all one. . . . Let us all unite. . . . Even the animals that eat people, even the people who keep the black magic that we do not like, let's embrace them all and be one people.

Although Chief Makuei speaks of the black skin, the unity of man and his universe is envisaged to embrace mankind in all its multiplicity of races and cultures. According to Chief Stephen Thongkol, people were initially created with racial and cultural uniformity. Language diversity later resulted from a punishment God imposed on man when he became so arrogant that he wanted to build a tower high enough to reach God in the sky.

When God saw them do this, he thought of something to bring confusion to their heads: he gave the people a very heavy sleep. They slept for a very, very long time. They slept for so long that they forgot the language they had used to speak. When they eventually woke up from their sleep, each man went his own way, speaking his own tongue. None of them could understand the language of the other any more. That is how people dispersed all over the world. Each man would walk his way and speak his own language and another would go his way and speak in his own language.

So our fathers used to tell us that all mankind, white or black, are one people; the division came when God gave people different languages after that long sleep. . . . That is the way God created us. God did not create people in different kinds; they were created as one kind.

And according to Chief Pagwot Deng, "All human beings who speak were created by the same creator in the same way. But God then gave each man his own ways and each man his words. We, the black people, have our own ways, but we cannot say that people are not related. All human beings who speak are related."

Since it is God who creates and destroys all mankind, the Dinka believe that mankind as a totality is subject to the same power of God, but at the same time they recognize that different peoples have different divinities and different religions. For instance, it is said that the Arab has his "God" and the European his "God." As a corollary to this localization of the concept of God, it is understood that the exclusive Dinka divinities do not have much power over Arabs, Europeans, or, to a lesser extent, the educated Dinka. Likewise, exclusive Arab and European gods do not have much power over the Dinka. The Over-All God, however, has power over all. By the same token, every human being, no matter what his race or religion, has a sanctity and a moral or spiritual value that must be respected. To wrong him is to wrong God himself and therefore invite a curse. Some people, notably divine chiefs and priests or other religiously inspired people, may possess the effective power to curse which the Dinka express as "bitterness," *kec,* a term which in its English translation coincidentally indicates the association between the power to curse and the origin of that power in the bitterness felt about a wrong. But while the bitterness of the wronged person results in an expressed curse and creates a chain of causation which might aggravate the guilt felt by the wrongdoer and therefore his self-punishment, conceived as imposed by God or lesser spirits, a curse for wrongdoing is supposed to be provoked by the mere fact of the wrongful act and is effective even if the wrong is unknown to the wronged. The power is believed to be intrinsic in the human "flesh" and is operative independently of the intentions of the wronged. Conceiving the South-North problem as rooted in the ethnocentrism of Northerners and their underestimation of Southerners, Chief Thon Wai spoke words which are relevant to Dinka theology.

> A man created by God with two legs and two eyes, who urinates and goes to the forest [to empty his bowels], cannot be considered a fool. He is a human being, a part of the human race. Even the tree which cannot speak has the nature of a human being. It is a human being to God, the person who created it. Do not despise it; it is a human being.
>
> Our brothers thought that we should be treated that way because we were in their eyes like fools. I have never heard of a man being such a fool. A human being who speaks with his mouth cannot be such a fool. Whatever way he lives, he remains a human being. And whatever he does must be thought of as the behavior of a human

being. If you see a man walking on his two legs, do not despise him; he is a human being. Bring him close to you and treat him like a human being. That is how you will secure your own life. But if you push him onto the ground and do not give him what he needs, things will spoil and even your big share, which you guard with care, will be destroyed.

This sensitivity to God's entire work shows the religious devotion of the Dinka and the richness of the moral content of their religion. According to the Seligmans, "The Dinka, and their kindred the Nuer, are by far the most religious peoples in the Sudan."[5] As Lienhardt has observed:

> God is held ultimately to reveal the truth and falsehood, and in doing so provide a sanction for justice between men. Cruelty, lying, cheating and all other forms of injustice are hated by God, and the Dinka suppose that, in some way, if concealed by men, they will be revealed by him. . . . God is made the final judge of right and wrong, even when men feel sure that they are in the right. God is then the guardian of faith—and sometimes signifies to man what really is the case, behind or beyond their errors of falsehood.
>
> The Dinka have no problem of the prospering sinner, for they are sure that Divinity will ultimately bring justice. Since among them every man at some time must meet with suffering or misfortune, death or disease among his family or his cattle, there is always evidence, for those who wish to refer to it, of Divine justice. It is a serious matter when a man calls on Divinity to judge between him and another, so serious that only a fool would take the risks involved if he knew he was in the

5. Charles G. Seligman, *The Pagan Tribes of the Nilotic Sudan* (London, G. Routledge & Sons, Ltd., 1932).

wrong, and to call upon Divinity as witness gives the man who does so an initial presumption of being in the right.[6]

Chief Thon Wai reflected the Dinka view when he said:

> Even if a right is hidden, God will always uncover the right of a person. It doesn't matter how much it might be covered; even if the covering be heaped as high as this house and the right is there, it will appear. It may be covered for ten years, and God will uncover it for ten years, until it reappears. . . . If a man is not given his right, God never loses sight of the right.

Dinka respect for the work of God and in particular for the essential equality of the human race calls for explanation in view of their complex attitude toward women and their ethnocentric view of themselves as essentially superior to other peoples. As I indicated earlier, the subordination of women to men is an outcome of the patrilineal orientation of Dinka society. It is unequivocally espoused by the Dinka without the least doubt of its validity. The story of how Chief Arol's father was freed from slavery by being exchanged with his sister is illustrative of this procreational stratification.

> My grandfather spoke and said, "If I remain with two girls, it is of no use. It is better that they take a girl, if they will accept. So I shall offer them one of the girls so that I may have my son back. One day, if my son survives, all will be well. But if it is a girl, a girl is only for sale; she is sold for cattle [in marriage]."

In the various versions of the myth of creation, God is said to have subsequently created the woman in response to man's request and used his rib. Chief Stephen Thongkol recounted the myth with a flare of sentimentality: "It is said that one

6. Lienhardt, *Divinity and Experience*, pp. 46–47.

rib was taken out of the man while he was asleep and used in making the woman. This is why, up to this day, when a man sleeps with a woman, she likes to put her hands on the man's ribs in his chest. She holds the man's chest, where she came from."

As we have already seen, a number of myths hold women responsible for the original sin which brought suffering and death upon man. Chief Pagwot Deng went as far as saying that "God almost decided not to create the woman." On the same myth, Chief Makuei ended his account with the remarks: "And when this came to pass, the snake came to crawl and the woman became what she is." Referring to how the snake persuaded the woman to eat the forbidden fruit, Chief Thon Wai remarked, "Hers was the small heart of a woman which easily changes." In answer to my query about the reason that provoked the woman who threw the potsherd into the river and requested from God that people die and never return, Chol Adija implied that it was a senseless act in keeping with the nature of women: "She was just angry; it is these ways of women, as you know them."

The Dinka consider women essentially jealous and prone to fanning hostilities which endanger group solidarities and often provoke destructive conflicts between group members. The story told by Chief Akot Awutiak about the manner in which his ancestress influenced her son to lie in favor of her brother as against her husband—the father of her son— is typical. The father cursed the boy to death in punishment and, as he was their only son, the wife abandoned the tribe and headed for the wilderness where some spiritual being caused her to become pregnant and give birth to a spiritually powerful son who later became the leader of his people— a complex cycle of wrong, punishment, fission, and fusion.

The Dinka do not, of course, associate women's divisiveness and jealousy with the inferior position they occupy in their society and all the injustices the system imposes upon them. While polygyny is taken for granted by both men and women, and the fidelity of women highly emphasized, the Dinka do not see any justification for co-wife rivalry and jealousy, which deeply affect the relations not only among the co-wives themselves and between them and their husband, but also between the women and the children, whether their own or those of their co-wives, and between the children themselves, whether full- or half-blood. Again, as women do not find avenues equally open for them to voice their grievances in the ordinary manner acceptable from men, they must of necessity resort to discreet and occasionally rebellious, if only ritualistic, ways of influencing situations. Rather than see justification, men devise more stringent ways of countervailing the negative role of women and especially their disharmonizing influence and impact on human relationships.

Dinka attitudes about women are complex, however, for, despite their subordination, women are highly regarded in connection with the value of procreation and wield considerable influence if only because of their close ties with children through crucial phases of child-rearing. During the nursing period, which may last for two or three years, the father is not only distant from the baby but is prohibited from having sexual relations with the nursing wife. This, together with the fact that in polygynous families the father's attention and affection are often shared and diffused within a wide circle, make the mother more reliable for the needed care and affection, and hence a stronger influence on the child. She is thus seen as a threat and the male society deems it necessary to be even more repressive, often with the acquiescence and even active support of the women themselves.

A child is encouraged from the earliest age to express affection for the father and never for the mother. While he must address his father as "Father" and never by his name, he calls his mother by her name and would be ridiculed and embarrassed if he referred to her as "Mother." While it is unthinkable for a Dinka child to be rude to his father, it is common for a child and desirable for a son to be in a domineering position vis-à-vis the mother; except in the most flagrant cases, the attribute of disobedience or obstreperousness toward the mother is tolerated and even admired.

All these rules are sanctioned and in effect cultivated by the mother. While a father can fatally curse a son who wrongs him, mothers are said to incapacitate themselves ritually from the time of their babies' birth, thereby divesting themselves of the spiritual power to curse their children, whatever the degree of wrong and whatever their bitterness.

While these norms superficially indicate the subordination of women, they also paradoxically show their pivotal role behind the screens of the male-dominated life-theater. Indeed, it is revealing to know that while the woman herself is not permitted to curse, the spiritual power of her agnatic kin, and especially her brother and father, over her children is supposed to be uniquely effective. It is easy to see how the close sentiments between mother and child extend to her family—mother, father, brothers, and sisters. Usually the child is most spoilt in those circles. Since the spiritual power to curse is usually embodied in guilt, it is expected to be strongest where emotional loyalty or involvement is greatest. And since society permits only males to resort to such methods, it is easy to see how the potential guilt feelings for wrongs against the mother are associated with wrongs against her relatives. And in any case, since the children are emotionally more attached to them than to their own agnatic kin with whom there is only greater rational attachment, the spiritual power of the former over the latter must logically be superior. Ultimately, the issue of the relative superiority or inferiority of either of the sexes becomes intricate and complex, despite the superficial pronouncements of the Dinka about women. Indeed, even these pronouncements

concern specific charges against women, but never judge on
the issue of superiority or inferiority in a categorical sense.

The Dinka view of racial stratification is also seemingly
simplistic but paradoxically complex, especially in the light
of their intensifying interaction with the outside world and
their increasing realization of the advantages some other
races and cultures have over them. On the first issue, what
I have termed the superficial view has been easily noted by
most observers of Dinka society, and consists of the dogmatic
assertion that whatever the distinctive merits of other races
or cultures, the Dinka represent the standard of what is
ideally human and therefore best. Others may have superior
technology or greater wealth in monetary terms, but all
things considered, Dinkaland is the most beautiful, the Dinka
race the perfect example of creation, Dinka cattle the ideal
wealth, and Dinka ways the best models of dignity.

The basic principle behind Dinka ethnocentrism is not so
much one of comparative merit and superiority over others,
it is that they regard themselves as distinct, unique, and all
things considered, content and unenvious, indeed, perhaps
envied. Chief Pagwot's words, in which he emphasized that
God created all peoples but gave each people their own
distinctive attributes is a good illustration of the point.
While he considered the institution of marriage as something
God ordained for the Dinka, he added that non-Dinka do not
marry, implying that whatever their marital customs, as long
as they do not follow formalities similar to those of the
Dinka, theirs was not marriage properly so-called. A number
of versions of the original myths also refer to cattle and
Dinka devotion to them with pride as God's favor to the
Dinka and linked to the very survival of the Dinka race, not
only in terms of livelihood but also in procreational terms.
According to Chief Stephen:

> When it comes to our ways, we the Dinka, God gave us
> something called cattle. Cattle are what we hold above

all things. We hold them as important as our own lives. And if a man has cattle, he marries a wife, and his wife bears him children and he names his children, some of them after cattle.

Chief Ayeny Aleu sees cattle as fundamental valuables for which others envy the Dinka.

It is for cattle that we are liked, we the Dinka. The government likes us because we keep cattle. All over the world people look at us because of cattle. And when they say "Sudan," it is not just because of our color, it is also because of our wealth; and our wealth is cattle. . . . It is because of cattle that people of all the tribes look to us with envy.

According to the myths of creation, the Dinka chose the cow in preference to the thing called "What," which God had offered as an alternative to the cow, but which the Dinka dismissed without even seeing. According to Loth Adija:

God asked man, "Which one shall I give you, black man; there is the cow and the thing called 'What,' which of the two would you like?"
The man said, "I do not want 'What.'"
Then God said, "But 'What' is better than the cow!"
The man said, "No."
God said, "If you like the cow, you had better taste its milk first before you choose it finally."
The man squeezed some milk into his hand, tasted it, and said, "Let us have the milk and never see 'What.'"[7]

To the Dinka, it is not just the idea of the cow but the particular breeds that exist in their world and the entire

7. "What" could be conceptually associated with curiosity and the search for scientific knowledge and inventiveness. The Dinka concept of knowledge emphasizes social norms and cultural continuity rather than scientific and technical knowledge. Hence, the rationalization of Dinka scientific and technical backwardness in comparison to Europeans and Arabs.

cattle complex which give their culture its distinctive character. Other peoples may have cattle, but they are not the same as Dinka cattle, and just as the Dinka are a distinctive race, so are their cattle in relation to those of others. Furthermore, even if their cattle be desirable in some respects, other peoples do not treat cattle with the reverence and the dignity which the Dinka show their cattle. It is because of the distinctiveness and the preference the Dinka give cattle that a man who acquires an ox of non-Dinka breed will usually include in the traditional ox songs by which men honor their oxen some insulting references, associating the ox with the undesirable ways of the race of its origin.

The pride of the Dinka in the distinctiveness of their cattle is implicit in Giirdit's reference to the color of the original sacred bull which the legendary character, Longar, is said to have sacrificed to bless the people and distribute the divine power inherent in its meat. In his words, "The bull was *mangok* [tawny], and this is a bull the Jur [other races] did not have. It is a special color-pattern for our race."

Chief Pagwot Deng was even more elaborate in expressing ethnocentrism through symbolism.

> We and the Arabs, we came from one place in creation. But when we came out of the Byre of Creation, we came with a white cow. And the Arabs had a brown cow. We also had a bull of our own—our pied bull [pied being the most senior color for the Dinka]. This pied bull served this white cow of ours and the white cow gave birth. When our white cow gave birth, the Arab brought his brown cow. Our people said, "This cow of yours, we will not allow our bull to serve." He had to take it back. That cow of his was impregnated by a brown snake. His cattle now have mottled sides because of the brown snake which served his cow.

Another feature which is mentioned in the interviews, as

distinctive of the Dinka and associated with creation, is the spears, the most important of which are the sacred spears embodying the divine authority of chieftainship. While chiefs are supposed to be men of peace and against the spilling of blood, their sacred spears are symbols of their coercive power to curse while the ordinary spears give the Dinka the weapon for their secular military coercion. As against an outside aggressor, the two sets of spears are combined in that the divine chief blesses the warriors with his sacred spear and points it at the enemy to subdue them spiritually. According to Chief Arol Kacwol, it was "the people of the spears, the Dinka and the other black men," who were "the first to come out" of creation. "Black people came out with their blackness and their spears. The others remained and were later given their own strength like writing. These are the things that were later given to the people who were left behind. But spears were the first to be given to man."

Of course, the widening of the concept of "black" is, at least in part, the outcome of the more recent movement to broaden nationalism to embrace at least the non-Arab tribes of the South. In the Ngok Dinka myths concerning the leadership of the Pajok clan and their acquisition of the sacred spears from the Byre of Creation, both the original consciousness of black identity and its more recent national-ist extensions emerge strongly. The theme of the sacred spears pervades all the accounts of the Ngok, but this version from Bulabek Malith of the Pajok clan is illustrative.

> When we came from the Byre, where people were cre-
> ated, there was a great man, an elder called Jok, who is
> our Founding Father. He was the man who led the peo-
> ple. He is now known as Jok, the Breaker-Through. . . .
> God gave Jok the sacred spear . . . with which our people
> used to take an oath. It was God who gave it to our
> ancestor, Jok, and said, "This spear belongs to all the
> black peoples of the world."

God created all of us together with the Arabs, but we are black and the spear that God gave us we do not point at black people to this day. Even if we fight with black people today, we will not ritually point the sacred spear at them, we the people called the Ngok.

Chief Ayeny Aleu goes even farther in his projection of black nationalism.

We look back, and the day people emerged we cannot tell. We do not know about it. But it seems that people came from there [the east] and they came across here [to the west]. . . . It is these people, the white people, who were the first to open the country. Those who went ahead became clever and opened their eyes to some things. Then they returned and claimed, "These were my brothers that I had left behind. I am now going back to join them." But our people had opened their eyes and that is now why those black Americans are fighting. Those black Americans who are fighting are our own people. The son of my grandmother, called Ayeny, was captured a long time ago. Who knows, maybe his family are among the people now said to be black Americans.

Implicit in this extension of nationalism in defense of black identity and tradition is the threat the Dinka and their fellow Southerners felt against themselves and their cultures in the context of today's Sudan and the predominance of the Arabized North. As is apparent in the quotation from Bulabek Malith, perhaps the strongest defense of tradition against Arab incursions comes from the Ngok Dinka who, paradoxically, have been in contact with the Arabs for centuries and have curiously combined the preservation of their identity as Dinka with a subtle process of adopting and assimilating Arab cultural elements. With the recent civil war and the complexities of their border problems as Southerners under Northern administration, a heightened degree of bitterness and apprehension for the future has emerged and with it a more vocal defense of tradition. Acueng Deng considers adherence to tradition as the ultimate guarantee of the survival of the Dinka.

> The suffering of the people is such that even as we sit here today, it continues; it has not ended. It will not end. But if people continue to endure, this suffering will one day come to an end. The ancient word has not been abandoned. To abandon it is what brings disaster. That is why the Oath Ashes[8] are now finishing the people by death.

Chief Biong Mijak, addressing himself to the question of prospects for national integration between the South and the North, was not only more extreme but also expressed appreciation of the separatist policies of British rule.

> This question of how people will live together with the Arabs, or whether people will mix or remain separate—why should we not remain separate? Why should we not remain as we are? We are now together, but each man has remained with his own color. We say those people are brown and we are black. God did not create at random. He created each people with their own kind. He created some people to live long and some people to die young: and he created some people brown and some black. We cannot say we want to destroy what God has created; all this is in God's hands. Even God would get angry if we spoiled his work. This is a God whom our white rulers revered. The English saved our country. . . .

8. The Dinka swear on the ashes of the cow-dung from the cattle of the chiefly lineages, which are believed to be sacred. Perjury is believed to cause death. An oath must therefore be administered by the legitimate authority with great caution and after extensive investigation of the facts. What is meant here is that its reckless administration by those traditionally unauthorized can have disastrous consequences.

If you, our children, have survived, hold to the ways of our ancestors very firmly. Let us be friends with the Arabs, but each man should have his own way. We are one Sudan, but let each man be by himself.

As the Dinka grapple with their relative position in the world complex of cultures and technological revolution, their mythology is beginning to react in an attempt to explain the contemporary realities of the Dinka world. We have already seen Chief Arol Kacwol's reference to the Dinka being created first with the spear and some people being created subsequently and given their own strength such as writing. But there are even more complex myths for harmonizing the traditional superiority complex of the Dinka and their subordination to other peoples which they now recognize. One such myth is told by Bulabek Malith and Loth Adija with only small variations. According to Bulabek:

> What our grandfathers used to say, and our ancestor, Jok, is said to have said is that when man was created, it was as twins. One was a brown child and one was a black child. The woman would keep the black child to herself, away from the father. Whenever the father came to see the children, she would present the brown child and keep the black child because she loved the black child very much. The man then said, "This child whom you keep away from me, in the future, when they [the children] grow up, I will not show him my secrets." That has remained a curse on us. It is because of this story which we have been told by our fathers that we have been deprived. Our father did not show us the ways of our ancestors fully. . . . It was the woman who kept her black child away from his father. Otherwise, we would have known more things than we know.

The second version of the myth as told by Loth speaks of triplets and includes the white race. While the main teller is Loth, the other elders present in the interview were eager to contribute, and did in fact contribute to the story in a manner which illustrates both how widely known the story is and the degree of contemporary significance the Dinka now see in it.

In the words of creation, it used to be said that when God created people, man was the first to be created. He was created from clay. And then God gave it breath and it became man. The woman was created subsequently. Then God said, "You two will bear children this way."
Then the woman gave birth to triplets. God made one child white and made one child brown and made one child black. This black child, his mother loved most. She would hide him from the man. The other children were the ones she showed her husband. Those were the only children that the man knew. One day, he found the woman suckling the black child. He said, "Whose child is this?"
She said, "He is my child."
He said, "And why do you hide the child? Is he of a separate birth or is he of our joint birth?"
She said, "He is of our joint birth."

Here, Marieu Ajak interjected, "They were triplets." Chol Adija added, "Then he said, 'This child you are hiding.'" Loth resumed the story and continued: "Yes, he said, 'This child of yours whom you hide will one day be the slave of these other children.' The white child was not really breast-fed. He merely sucked on the breasts after they had been emptied. So he was the child his father took."
Acueng Deng interjected, "Whenever people went into public gatherings, she would prevent her black child from going. Only the white child would go with his father." Loth resumed and continued the narration.

Yes! This white child, his father thus maintained him; he looked after him very well. As he was prevented from sucking, his father took good care to feed him. He took a gourd, a new fresh gourd, bored a hole in the gourd and emptied it. The child was very hungry. The father of the child raised his hands to the sky and prayed, "God, is there nothing for you to give to this son of mine?" That gourd was filled with milk. That white son of his drank the milk. This white son he took to God to be the servant of God. That is said to be how the English went away and learned. Arab and Dinka remained; the brown Arab remained with the Dinka with their mother. It was said that their mother was the mother of all people.

As some of the myths already cited have indicated, there is a striking similarity between Dinka religious mythology and the stories of the Bible and the Koran. Among the many such stories or myths which appeared in the interviews are: How God created man from mud and the woman from the rib of the man; how the woman was tempted by the snake to eat the forbidden fruit; how God punished mankind in consequence; how a divine leader made waters part so that his people might cross; how a prophet was born of a woman without a biological father; the miracles performed by that prophet and his religious message to the world.

Perhaps the account of this last myth, although told by Chief Makuei Bilkuei in a disjointed manner, will illustrate the close interconnections between Dinka mythology and religion and those of the Bible.

Later on, Deng of the sky sent word. He stopped a girl from giving birth. Her menstrual period also stopped. Then that girl suddenly became pregnant without sleeping with a man. She became pregnant from the wind.

When the morning star saw it, he sent word, "The day I come down, that is the day this child will be born."

Her father and mother asked her, "Where did you get the child?"

She said, "I don't know."

Then the star came down. That is when the child was born. A big chief had said, "The day the child is born we should hear it."

So, when the child was born, the chiefs came with a big ram to make a sacrifice for the child who was born.

At that time, a big army came crossing the country. The little baby started to talk and said, "Mother, take me away from here." That was the child who brought the book, the word of God. That child was taken away and then the whole country was slaughtered. They were all slaughtered and killed.

Then he began to teach people and he was followed. And when people crossed the river, the army of the chief which was after him could not cross and his army drowned behind. That is how the enemy disappeared. That is how the Red Sea came to be known as the Red Sea. He brought the stone with him. That was the man who brought death and who brought life.

Then the man died and he was buried. Three days afterward he got up. In one place he found a woman crying and he said to the woman who was crying, "What are you crying about?"

She said, "My child is dead."

"Where?"

"Here."

He took a small stick and tapped the dead child and the child woke up alive.

And then they were drinking beer. The ancient people sat and drank their beer. When the beer was finished the people made a wish, "Oh, if only this pot could get full again!" That man came and said, "Pour water into the pot." The pot became full of beer and people drank the beer. That was the man who started to teach people the word of God.

When I asked Chief Makuei what this man was called, he

gave me a mispronunciation of the Arabic for Jesus and went on to give other Biblical names in Arabic, "That man was called Issu; Issu was his name. And the original father of the people was Adam and his wife was Hawa. Those were the original people who started the world." In a totally separate context, the Ngok elders gave the same names. Loth Adija was the first to mention the name of the original mother in Arabic as Awo (Hawa); Chol Adija quickly agreed, "Yes, her name was Awo." Loth then said, "And the father of the children was Adam; his name was Adam." To my question, "Are these the names the Dinka actually mention?" Loth said, "Yes, those are the names the Dinka mention. Very old men used to say so." And Marieu Ajak added, "Elders of the past used to say that."

Although the anthropologists who have studied the Nilotics do not give accounts of these myths from Nilotic sources, their description and analysis of Dinka and Nuer religions attest to the similarities between them and the ancient Middle-Eastern religions.[9] Indeed, Professor Evans-Pritchard has gone as far as making the following observation:

> I am, of course, well aware that Nuer religion is very unlike what we know in general about Negro religions. One cannot even say that it is a typical Nilotic religion. It is certainly very unlike the religion of the Anuak, of the Luo of Kenya, of the Acholi, of the Alur, or of the Shilluk. Indeed, only the religion of the Dinka can be said to have strongly marked affinities with it, and it can be further said that in some respects the religions of these two peoples resemble less other Negro religions than some of the historic religions. They have features which bring to mind the Hebrews of the Old Testament. Professor C. G. Seligman clearly sensed this, as his ac-

9. For Dr. Lienhardt's brief references to Dinka creation myths see *Divinity and Experience*, p. 40.

count of the Dinka and Nuer shows; and Miss Ray Huff-
man, an American Presbyterian missionary who spent
many years among the Nuer, remarks that "the missionary feels as if he were living in Old Testament times,
and in a way this is true." When, therefore, I sometimes
draw comparisons between Nuer and Hebrew conceptions, it is no mere whim but is because I myself find it
helpful, and I think others may do so too, in trying to
understand Nuer ideas to note this likeness to something
with which we are ourselves familiar without being too
intimately involved in it.[10]

Throughout his book, Evans-Pritchard goes beyond this
general observation to point out, as also does Lienhardt
about the Dinka, specific examples of similarities with the
Old Testament.[11]

It may of course be argued that the myths are not authentically Nilotic, but versions of the Bible stories recently adopted from the missionaries. That was indeed my first reaction
when the first chief told versions of the myths of creation. I
was so convinced that he was relating somewhat distorted
Bible stories that I was hardly interested in what he had to
say except as evidence of change. But as he elaborated and
as I began to hear more versions of a similar nature from
other chiefs, the issue began to pose more questions I could
not dismiss lightly. For instance, these chiefs are men in
their seventies or sixties, the youngest in their forties. They
all prefaced or concluded their stories with the assertion that
they had heard the stories from their grandfathers and

10. Edward Evans-Pritchard, *Nuer Religion* (Oxford, Clarendon Press, 1956),
p. vii.
11. It is interesting that, in blessing a person, the Dinka pour cool river water into
a fresh gourd container and, after spraying some of the water into the sky, wet
five spots on the body of the person being blessed—the forehead, the spot of the
upper chest close to the base of the neck, the palms of both hands, and the backs
of both feet. These spots resemble both the wounds of crucifixion and the sign
of the cross.

fathers which would extend the life span of the stories even further. The modern missionary presence among the Dinka is closely associated with the colonial presence, which was not well entrenched in many areas until the 1920s and '30s. It seems most unlikely that people who, by virtue of their age during the advent of missionary influence in the area, had already consolidated their conception of Dinka mythology could still be so formative as to adopt and integrate foreign concepts into their own myths at so late a time and then be in a condition to mislabel the myths as having been told them by their seniors. There can be little doubt that the origin of the myths goes beyond the recent history of missionary influence in Dinka society.

When I mentioned to the Ngok elders in general terms the similarities I had found between the Dinka myths of creation and the stories in Holy Books, posing the possibility of the Dinka having adopted them from the Europeans and the Arabs, Bulabek Malith told the story of creation in terms identical to what I had already heard from many people and the factual details of which I had not introduced to him, and then concluded the story by addressing himself to the comparative point I had posed: "This is not the word of education. I heard it from my elders. I did not find it in the books [he is illiterate]. Elders told us that."

It is interesting that the literate chiefs to whom the stories were clearly introduced by the Christians and the Muslims do not at all refer to them. Of course, this might mean that they are too aware of the foreign origin of the myths to attribute them to the Dinka. But when Chief Lino Aguer was told of the versions given by the illiterate chiefs and was asked as to whether he thought they were adopted from Christian or Muslim sources, he gave an explanation which would suggest either the coincidence or the unity of human experience or a dynamic process in which the Dinka themselves influenced the written word. Whether he meant the local books

written by the missionaries or the text of the Bible is somewhat ambiguous.

> What the people you talked to were saying was the word
> of God. The missionaries came and found that the people
> already knew a lot. The missionaries actually wrote down
> what they heard from elders. What is in the Holy Book
> was what was recorded from the people. It is just that our
> people did not know how to write. We grew up hearing it
> from our fathers, sons from the fathers, coming down to
> us from well back. What was lacking was somebody to
> write it down and say, "This is our Grandfather's book
> and our Father's book." That was what was missing. But
> the word of mouth which we ourselves heard was there.

Whether this is just the coincidence of human experience
or a cultural diffusion of honored concepts, there is every
reason to believe that the Nilotic peoples were not isolated
from the sources of these universal religions. Evidence from
both contemporary Dinka society and the antiquities from
Ancient Egypt would tend to confirm incidents of cross-
cultural influence. It has been suggested, for instance, that
the Dinka practice of training the horns of their bulls to grow
according to the tastes of the owner might also have existed in
ancient Egypt, judging from Egyptian paintings. Similarly,
paintings suggest that Egyptians adorned their bulls with
decorations and displayed them in a manner quite similar to
the Dinka practice. Even more relevant to religious expression is the similarity of the burial rites pertaining to the
divine leaders of the Nilotics and those of ancient Egyptian
kings. After all, the history of both Christianity and Islam
in the Sudan goes back to the early centuries of the emer-
gence of these religions. Their extension into Dinka country
would be by no means surprising.

While the myths themselves are ancient in their origin,
certain details in their contents might have originated in the

more recent contacts with the outsiders. That is why, when I asked the elders what the names of the original man and woman were, they gave me Awo, a mispronunciation of the Arabic name for Eve, Hawa, as "H" does not exist in the Dinka alphabet. The same was the case in the version of the myth relating to Jesus, where the Arabic for Jesus, Issa, was also mispronounced as Issu. In the attempt to adapt these ancient myths to current situations, the Dinka might have developed a tendency to use the names of the counterparts in Christian or Muslim stories. It is possible that an educated youth tells an elder, who gives the Dinka account of a myth, that according to Christians and Muslims the same story exists though the names of the principals differ. In order to make the myth more understandable to a Christian or a Muslim, that elder could introduce the Christian or Muslim names in the same Dinka version through a kind of myth-translation into a foreign culture.

It is also quite possible that the names too have a more distant origin and, as they tend to be based on the Arabic versions, they must have resulted from a Coptic or Muslim influence rather than from the recent Western Christian missionary work in the area.

In a word then, Dinka creation-myths purport to explain the origins not only of the Dinka world but also of the inclusive world known to the Dinka. Since the participants in this embracing map have not been exclusively Dinka, a degree of cross-cultural influence is to be expected and does in fact occur with respect to the Judaic, Christian, and Islamic traditions. The accounts of the chiefs and elders that are included in this book give a penetrating lead into the comparative fabric of Dinka religion and culture.

Leadership

As with the myths of creation, the dynamics of tradition are clearly marked in the history of leadership which is often

embodied in myths that the Dinka tell with notable partiality. Every chiefly family tends to view the history of their
territorial group in terms of their genealogy even though
they might have come into chieftainship at a relatively late
stage. Even the few lineages who are indisputably known to
have held leadership from the original phases of Dinka
history have conflicting claims for supremacy. Even the
myth concerning Ayuel Longar, who is said to have been
the original chief, is not lacking in controversy resulting
from competing claims of descent from him or against his
original paramountcy. Some versions speak of two mythical
characters with the name Ayuel, one being the original leader
and the other an impostor of one sort or another. A lineage
may claim both association with the original Ayuel and victory over the other Ayuel. Yet others claim victory over
the original Ayuel who, in acknowledgment of their competing power, gave them a share in his divine chieftainship while he retained paramount authority.

In *Divinity and Experience,* Dr. Lienhardt quotes a number
of versions which have as their central theme an acceptance
of Ayuel as the first to be created by God and the original
divine leader of the Dinka, who, at the same time, displayed
a destructive attribute, predominantly that of spearing people
in the river, and from whom the people are eventually
redeemed, almost invariably by the founding ancestor of
whomever narrates the myth—usually a member of one of
the chiefly lineages. There is therefore in these versions an
ambivalent attitude toward Ayuel Longar: he is considered a
spiritually inspired leader, as all divine chiefs of the Dinka
are supposed to be, and at the same time an engineer or agent
of what amounts to revolutionary evil, from which the divine
leaders of the Dinka are expected to redeem their people. But
since the paramountcy of Ayuel is also assumed, he is presented as eventually conferring his divine powers onto those
who subdue him and blessing them to be the leaders of the

Dinka. According to some versions, he then retains a remote supremacy over them while he allows them to conduct the everyday affairs of leadership.

Although many of the versions of the myth portray Longar as possessing both the spiritual powers of a divine leader and the evil attributes which the Dinka do not normally associate with divine chieftainship, some opinions which emerge in the versions of the myths I collected depict him as the Father of the Dinka and a religiously inspired leader with exceptional powers to bless, cure, and presumably curse to effect his divine authority. According to Chief Albino Akot, he was indeed the man who saved the Dinka from the powers which were spearing people in the river.

> They say there was a big spirit which killed people on the riverside. This spirit stayed on the riverside and would not allow people to cross. It was Longar who subdued this spirit. He fought until he killed this evil spirit which was frightening people and the people went across. That is how it happens in our stories. It is said that it was the spear that strengthened his power. Whatever illness there was, Longar would come and cure it. Diseased people were taken to him to save because he was a sacred man with spiritual powers, very strong powers. Nobody was like him.

Although Chief Akot does not claim Longar to be his ancestor, the myth he told about his ancestor, Tiak-Tiak, also known as Cakcak, is quite similar in parts to the myth of Longar in the version collected by Lienhardt among the Apuk tribe of the Rek.

> Long ago, lions used to hold dances, and a man called Jiel attended a lion's dance. A lion asked him for his bracelet [or ring] and when it was refused, the lion cut off his thumb in order to pull off the bracelet. As a result of this, Jiel died, leaving an old wife with a daughter but no

son. In bitter distress, she went to weep by the bank of the river. A Power of the river, Malengdit, came to her and asked her why she wept, and when she said that it was because her husband was dead and she had no son, the Power called her to him in the river. He told her to lift her skirt, and to draw the waves [or the foam] toward her with her hand so that they might enter her. He then gave her a spear [which if carried by a woman is a sign that she has borne a male child] and a fish to sustain her, and told her to go swiftly home, for she had conceived a son whom she would soon bear.

The woman went home and bore a male child whom she called Aiwel [Longar].[12]

Even as a baby, Aiwel (Ayuel) started to behave miraculously, though in secret. His conduct was eventually discovered by his mother whom he bade not to tell anyone or else she would die. But she told someone and she died.

Aiwel then left his mother's people and went to live with his father, the Power, in the river, and grew up there. When he was a grown-up man, he came back from the river with an ox which had in it every known color, but was predominantly *mangok*. . . . This was the ox by the name of which he was to be known henceforth: "Longar."[13]

The first part of Chief Akot's version about his ancestor mentions a certain Longar but is essentially about intra-familial tensions which led to the death of an only son and the desertion of his mother, that Longar's sister, who eventually comes across the Power that gives her a child.

Cakcak's own mother, Arek, was the wife of Majak. They had one child called Ajang. There was no other child;

12. Lienhardt, *Divinity and Experience*, pp. 171–72.
13. Ibid., p. 173.

Ajang was the only child of Arek. My grandfather had a lot of cattle. His brother-in-law called Longar, brother of Arek, also had many cattle. He came and stayed with his brother-in-law.

As the elders sat and played a game of *wet* [checkers], they talked. Longar said, "Majak, this lion which is finishing off people, if the two of us are really divine chiefs, why don't we pray and each one of us take his spear out to be used for killing this lion! The one among us who is the chief, his spear will kill the lion instantly."

It was a big lion which caught and ate people on the way. He said, "We will send Ajang." Ajang was the son of Longar's sister. Majak said, "Very well." Ajang was called, "Ajang, come, you are going to kill the lion."

He said, "How can I go and kill the lion alone?"

They said, "You will go; it is the chiefs who are sending you, big chiefs; nothing will happen to you. You will take two spears; there will be no third spear. Your father's spear is here; he will bless it with spit. He says you will kill the lion with it. Longar will also do the same to his spear; he will spit on his spear and will give it to you and you will go."

Ajang took the spears and went to hunt the lion. When he met the lion, he took out the spear of his maternal uncle. People had said, "If it is the spear of Longar which will kill the lion, all the cattle of Majak Yolker will be taken by Longar; nothing will remain. But if it is the spear of Majak Yolker which will kill the lion, then all the cattle of Longar will go to Majak." That was the bet that was made.

Of course, the child listens to his mother's word first of all. His mother talked to him and said, "Your uncle is not a chief; if all his cattle are taken, he will be poor. But your father has a lot of people; even if his cattle are taken, the clan of his father will collect cattle and he will be rich again."

He went, took out his maternal uncle's spear first and speared the lion with it. But it did not kill the lion. As the lion was approaching, he took his father's spear and speared it. He killed the lion instantly. Then he took the spears and went home to bring the message.

When he brought the message, his mother was waiting for him on the way. She said, "With whose spear did you kill the lion?"

And he said, "With my father's spear."

She said, "Oh no, no, do not say that again, please! Say it is your uncle's spear you used to kill the lion. My son, do not say what you just said. If you say it was the spear of your father with which you killed the lion, I will kill myself."

So the boy went home. The elders came and said, "Ajang, with whose spear did you kill the lion?"

His father too came and said, "With whose spear did you kill the lion?"

He said, "Father, it was with the spear of my uncle."

His father said, "No! Ajang, my son, is it true? Was it with your uncle's spear?"

He said, "Yes father, it was with my uncle's spear."

He said, "If it was your uncle's spear, so be it. You go and make the fire. Spread the cow dung to dry and make a smudge fire in the hearth. We will see at night."

They stayed. People stopped talking. Each man went his own way thinking that the cattle of Majak was gone. At night his father said, "We will sleep at the cattle hearth, you and I. If it is true that you used your uncle's spear to kill the lion, then you will wake up. If it is not, you will not wake up; you will die at night."

In the morning, when people woke up, Ajang was found stiff and dead.

From here, the story becomes essentially the same as the one leading to the myth of Longar, except that the character in the myth is Cakcak and not Longar.

His mother ran away into the forest. She went into the wilderness. Then she went and found Malengdit who stopped her in the river. He was a man of the river. She entered the river, wanting to cross, but she could not. And when she could not, she sat and cried on the bank of the river.

So Malengdit came and said, "Why do you sit crying all the time? What is the problem with you?"

And she said, "I have lost my only son. My son has died."

So he said, "There is no need for you to cross the river then. You stay here on this side of the river. You will return from here. What is disturbing you will be solved here. You hold the water to your bosom and you will have a child."

So she pushed the water close to her bosom. The foam of the river with which children used to play in the river came and entered her. She became pregnant.

When she was three months pregnant and it was definite that she was pregnant, she said to Malengdit, "What you said has come true."

And he said, "Well, if it has come true, you may now go home; you can return home. And if you go home, this child, name him Atiaktiak," meaning waves, the waves that brought the child, "and if you are asked, say, it is my great-grandfather Malengdit who gave me this child!"

So, that is how Atiaktiak came about. Arek went back and Atiaktiak was born. Atiaktiak came and started the clan and brought a new way of running the tribe. He became the substitute for Ajang who had died. Ajang had been an only child. So if Arek had not gone away to look for another child, they would have stayed without a child, and the cattle would have been taken away. Arek was the only wife, she was the single wife of Majak.

While there is the usual element of competition against

Longar, Akot claims no association between Ajang's maternal uncle and the great Longar. In answer to a question as to whether the Longar mentioned was the legendary Longar, he said:

> That I am not sure of. But I think the ancient Longar who was a powerful man feared by everybody is not this man Longar; the uncle of Ajang is a different man. He was a smaller Longar; nothing as great as the original Longar. The original Longar could not be challenged. Nobody could be braver than the original Longar. That was known to be the uniqueness of his power. It was Longar alone who was known for such great power. But this small Longar who came later on and who challenged Majak was a much more insignificant person. The original Longar was very much feared. He was a man who if he said a word against you, trouble would beset you without his seeing you.

And in any case, since, according to Akot's own account, Cakcak's father was supposed to have been captured by Arab slavers and then returned, and since Cakcak himself is said to have led his people against the Arab slave-traders in the nineteenth century, including Mahdists like Zubeir Pasha, his story and therefore his maternal uncle, Longar, could not be related to the period of the original Longar.

In some versions, Ayuel Longar is viewed as a competitor for chieftainship against another family or a half-brother with established authority. In a version somewhat similar to the version recorded by Dr. Lienhardt, Chief Thon Wai presents this theme.

> The ancient world was contested by Ayuel Longar and the family of Padiet, son of Diing. Those were the men who fought for the land. They were the sons of one father and two women; a man and his father's son.
> Dinka chieftainship was divided. One chieftainship

remained with Ayuel and the other with Padiet. Some became Kiec of Ayuel and others became Ric of Padiet.

So, how chieftainship started goes back a long way; it did not begin recently; it began in the ancient past. It began with our ancestors. Ayuel was in competition with Padiet. Ayuel sent a messenger to go and visit the camp of the Sun. And when the Sun saw him, they had a quarrel. He was given two plates full of food and told, "If you finish them, then you are a chief." When Padiet rejected his chieftainship, Ayuel Longar came and called all the other tribes together. Then he said, "This food we must finish. How can such a small plate defeat us?"

Thus he called his entire tribe and for four days they ate, but the plate was not emptied. They got tired and said, "What a terrible plate, a plate with dark anus. Throw it away." This, Chief Sun did not like.

Chief Sun was the first to be created. He said, "What should I do with this man? How shall I deal with him?" Ayuel Longar built for himself a cattle-byre with eight doors. When the Sun came in through one door, Ayuel hid himself on the other side. That way, he went around the cattle-byre, going from one door to another. That's what the man did, the man, Ayuel Longar. When the Sun entered the byre this way, Ayuel went that way. This went on for a while. At last the Sun got in touch with the Moon, and said, "Chief Moon, this thing has defeated me. The man called Ayuel throws away my things—the food that I sent him. And he is challenging me. What should we do?"

The Moon said, "Well, at night, when the world is dark, I shall come out. I will join them in a conversation, he and his family. He will be sitting with his wives and his children."

The Sun said, "Very well. What then?"

The Moon said, "I will spear his head."

He sent a spear from above and it thundered down and fell on Ayuel's head. That was how Chief Ayueldit was destroyed.

Then it was said that a cattle-byre should be built as a tomb for Ayuel. Ayuel spoke; he was not really dead. The spear which hit his head reached the ground, but was still in the sky. When the tribe attempted to dig out the spear it was not possible. So the cattle-byre was built on Ayuel while he was still alive. That was how Ayuel was buried and that's how there came to be a cattle-byre of Ayuel Longar. And that is how there came to be the clan of Ayuel Longar and the clan of Padiet. They stood next to one another. Ayuel's sect was ahead and Padiet's sect was next.

So that is how chieftainship first came to our land, the South. That is how it came to the Dinka. Indeed, it came to all people of the world.

The theme of competition is perhaps most explicit in the Ngok versions of the myth which subordinate Ayuel Longar, the founder of the Dhiendior clan, to Jok, the founder of the Pajok clan. Dhiendior, which means "women's clan," presumably derives from the fatherless status of Ayuel's birth which the Ngok themselves do not mention in their accounts. The theme of Ayuel's challenge to Jok and Jok's spiritual victory over him was repeated with consistency by the chiefs and elders I interviewed including representatives of both Pajok and Dhiendior.

I give the accounts of these versions in some detail because as Dr. Lienhardt's fieldwork did not extend into Ngok territory, his book does not contain the material I collected among them. It is also worth mentioning that the Ngok represent an interesting anomaly, as they have been in known contact with the Arabs for centuries and have assimilated certain elements of Arab culture, especially with respect to political authority and status, but have otherwise remained strikingly Dinka and have preserved much of classical Dinka traditions. As their versions of the leadership myths will show and as I will argue later, the consolidation of paramount authority, both traditional and modern, in the Pajok lineage has profoundly affected Ngok understanding of the origin of leadership. The Dhiendior too have consistently held the second most important position in both the traditional and modern systems, the latter beginning with the Turko-Egyptian confirmation and consolidation of the traditional hierarchy and authority. After tracing the history of Ngok leadership from Jok, Paul Howell, a British anthropologist whose fieldwork was done among the Nuer and the Ngok Dinka—both areas in which he served as District Commissioner during the Anglo-Egyptian condominium rule—observes, "The position has been held in this line ever since and according to strict primogeniture, the office descending to the eldest son of the eldest wife in each case."[14] Howell has also observed that "Such political power as is backed by the Government in the present system of administration was naturally accorded to the Chief of the spear by the Ngok themselves, and not only to the principal Pajok family, but also to the minor leaders who are all Chiefs of the spear, either of the Pajok clan or the Dhiendior."[15]

The manner in which the Pajok consistently maintained and reinforced their authority through the difficult nineteenth-century upheavals preceding the advent of British rule and the way they protected not only their own people, but also Southerners, Dinka and non-Dinka alike, through contacts with central authorities, is a recurrent theme in the accounts of the chiefs interviewed here from both the Ngok and the South. This theme will be elaborated in Chapter 3.

14. Paul Howell, "The Ngok Dinka," in *Sudan Notes and Records*, 32 (1951), 264.
15. Ibid.

In the present context, I confine my observations to the earlier period and the evidence for Pajok's claim to original leadership.

In the interview in which Chief Biong Mijak and Bulabek Malith recounted the myths of Pajok leadership, Chief Pagwot Deng, himself descended from the Dhiendior lineage, contributed to the myths; and his presence, we can assume, generated the moderation with which comparative reference was made to Longar. Also significant to the substance of the interviews is the political atmosphere which then prevailed, especially the anti-Arab sentiment and the black nationalism that had emerged.

According to Chief Biong Mijak:

> Because of the way we came from the Byre of Creation, what is now said about this [chieftainship], that it is to be started anew, is not correct. Things came this way from creation. . . . This Pajok clan and the Dhiendior clan came as chiefs from original times. . . . Jok was called Jok Athurkok [the Breaker-Through]. His name signified the man leading the way out of the Byre of Creation. He came from that way [the east], the way the Arabs face when they pray and we face when we slaughter our beasts in sacrifice. We face the same way, but we are different—we are Dinka. . . . So, this black world belonged to the Dinka from the beginning.

Bulabek Malith was more elaborate in his account of the circumstances leading to Jok's acquisition of chieftainship, emphasizing the theme of self-sacrifice which the Dinka attribute to their chiefs, and something of the peculiarities or abnormalities which are often associated with prophets or men of God.

> When we came from the Byre, where people were created, there was a great man, an elder called Jok, who is our Founding Father. He was the man who led the people. He

is now known as Jok Athurkok. It is what Jok left behind that I am going to relate to you. Jok said, "When I was in the lead, God told me, 'In all of this country, the man I will make to lead the people, I will take one eye from him; I will take one testicle from him; and I will kill a bull and make him carry the meat; and I will spear him on his foot and make him sleep with the spear on his foot.'" My ancestor said, "I will endure all that." He was speared on the foot; one testicle was taken off him; one eye was taken off him; God did that to him and he gave him a big load of meat to carry. At night he carried the meat on his head. In the middle of the night, he took all that meat and carried it where God wanted it to be taken. When God came in the morning, he asked, "Who carried all this meat?" And our ancestor said, "I did." God said, "I see. In that case, I will make you lead the people." That is why God put him ahead to lead the black people.

Bulabek then introduced the idea of the sacred spears explaining that God gave Jok the spears for the protection of all black peoples. Longar is then introduced as a co-leader.

And when he [Jok] left his people carrying these sacred spears, he said to his people that God had told him that a man called Longar would lead the people with him. "Longar will lead and you Jok will follow the people to protect them from behind. You will protect the people from a certain plague which will follow them, a plague which, if it reaches people, will never leave them again— it will always destroy your people." Jok named the plague; he said it was the cyclone. Cyclones would come and he would stop them.

Thus, what might have amounted to an admission of Longar's initial seniority is quickly counteracted with a theme that focuses and lays preeminence on the role of Jok as the one who was performing the vital function of protection from behind. The story continues to elaborate on Jok's protective role.

> Longar was in the lead. Then Longar found a woman called Ayak who stopped the people on the way. She said to Longar, "You cannot pass."
> So all the black people stopped because the woman had blocked their way. People who were being protected by Jok in the back stopped going forward. So Jok went through the crowds to see what had stopped the people from going forward. He found this woman who had sat in the path.
> Jok said, "Why? Longar, why have you stopped?"
> Longar said, "This woman has refused to let us pass."
> "What does she say?"
> "She says, 'I have this flour. If anybody steps on it, it will be bad.'"
> My grandfather went ahead. Jok went ahead and stepped on the flour of the woman, allowing people to pass. Then he told Longar to go ahead and lead the way. So, what Pagwot was saying before is true. Longar and Jok were the original leaders of the black people. They are the leaders to this day, as we are here now. Yes.

The narrator then goes back to the story to continue the theme of Jok's self-sacrifice for his people.

> When they came, they found a river which they could not cross. When this river stopped them, my ancestor, Jok, took out his daughter and decorated her and put her in the river. Then he said to Longar, "Spear that thing in the river." Longar took out his spear and speared a saddle which was in the river. The saddle broke his spear and the man who was on the saddle disappeared. The river dried up and the people crossed to the other side.

This last part of the myth recalls the point made by Albino
Akot and Lino Aguer that Longar was in fact not spearing
his people but a spirit which killed people on the riverside
and would not allow people to cross. This point is significantly at variance with the theme in almost all the versions
collected by Dr. Lienhardt which attribute to Longar an
evil-virtuous dualistic image.

Bulabek's version once more introduces the theme of
Longar's possible seniority, at least initially, but views it in
terms of Longar's unwarranted ambition in competition for
power. As in the version given by Chief Thon Wai, Ayuel is
here seen, perhaps figuratively, as Jok's brother or half-
brother. "When they were on the other side with his brother
Longar, Longar said, 'I will become the chief of the tribe.'
Jok accepted. He gave him the leadership and said, 'Very
well, you take the tribe; go ahead and lead them.'"

The story then takes a more historical turn and leaps into
more recent times. Apparently, Jok and his family remained,
heading some portions of the Dinka, while Longar proceeded
in his migration with other portions. But Jok's indispensability once more comes into the picture of those led by Longar.

Longar went leading the people who were continuing
their migration. But Longar found this difficult. We met
with the Arabs and people were fighting. So people held
a meeting. All the nine sections of the Ngok met and
decided to send their young men back. Young men of
the age-set called Kiec were sent. Longar said to them,
"Go back and fetch the son of Jok to come and attempt
the leadership in this war, to see whether he will succeed." So the age-set called Kiec returned to fetch the
son of Jok, who was the son of the great-grandson of
Jok, called Dongbek. Dongbek had Kon and Kwol, his
children. The elders of the tribe said to their young men,
"You go and bring Kon." On the way the age-set decided,

"We will not fetch Kon. Kon is older than us and if he comes, he will not treat us young men well. We will bring Kwol." When they arrived, Dongbek said to them, "What your elders told you was not Kwol, it was Kon. The elders told you to ask for Kon and not Kwol." They said, "Yes, but Kwol is the person we want." Dongbek accepted. He said, "Very well, you will go with Kwol. Kon will remain." Kon remained in the country of Lual Yak. He did not reach Ngokland. Only Kwol came.

According to a version I received in another context, Dongbek first refused to give Kwol to the age-set, arguing that he was too hot-tempered to be chief and urging them to accept Kwol's older brother. When the age-set persistently begged for Kwol, Dongbek, after counseling his son, blessed him and gave him the sacred spears of his ancestors and allowed him to lead the tribe. As they carried him away, they sang the following hymn which the Ngok still sing during the inauguration of the Paramount Chief:

> "Kiec, this is a flash of light to light
> your way."
> Dongbek thus honored us with Kwol,
> "May Kwol give you the life of my father,
> Bulabek."
> In the land of Bulabek
> we had no Chief to guide our way,
> no Chief to arrange our words.
> "Kiec, this is a flash of light to
> brighten your way."

The hot-temperedness of Kwoldit appears in a rather subsidiary myth about him which maintains that as he was being thus carried, a branch of a tree pricked him with thorns. He asked to be placed on the ground and uttered a curse on the tree in that area: "May you perish so that your thorns never

prick another person." According to the Ngok, the trees in
that area subsequently died, leaving a barren desert-like
territory which they claim still bears witness to the curse.

It is said that it was Kwol who defeated the Lueel and the
Arabs. Bulabek stressed only the Arabs as the enemy Kwol
defeated because of the atmosphere of hostility with the
North prevailing during the period of the interview.

> It is Kwol who made it possible for us to hold our coun-
> try up to this day. The coming of Kwol is what saved our
> people. Kwol bore his son, Monydhang, during the war
> with the Arabs. His father told him, "This spear, you
> hold it and use it, but never point it at the black man.
> God gave us this spear to be the guardian of all the
> black people. If you fight with the Arab, point it at the
> Arab; he is your enemy. But the black peoples are not
> your enemies." Kwol fought the war with the Arabs.
> It is he who brought safety to this day. That is why our
> people are in their present territory.

Bulabek's mention of Longar being initially in the lead and
his sending for Jok's descendants must be confusing to someone not used to Dinka genealogical and even historical leaps.
Genealogical details of intervening names are important, but
the designation of the whole line and of individual principals
by the names of the more preeminent ancestors in the line is
also customary. Likewise, the reference to sections of the
Ngok should be seen as figurative rather than a reflection of
the true situation then, as the structure and the political
organization of the Ngok had not yet established itself the
way it is today.

That the period and even the personalities in the account
by Bulabek are interfused or confused is apparent from
another strand of the myth of the competition between Jok
and Longar in which Longar's power is defeated by Jok's
forcing Longar to relinquish his claim to leadership. The

dynamics here vary from the theme of Longar or his descendants first leading and then surrendering on discovering the
formidability of leadership. According to this strand, which
Bulabek himself added to his account, Longar relinquished
his leadership to Jok so that the possibility of Longar's descendants sending the tribe to fetch Jok's descendant becomes anomalous.

> Longar wanted to try to win chieftainship. What our
> ancestor said is that he wanted to test him. He had a bull
> called Mangar. He sharpened the horns of that bull and
> whenever the cattle were released, he stained the horns
> with blood. Whenever his bull fought with other bulls,
> he won and killed those bulls. Thus, he finished all the
> bulls of the cattle-camp. When his bull had killed the
> bulls of the camp, Longar came to Jok and said, "Jok,
> my father's son, tomorrow let our bulls fight; let them
> play." Jok accepted. Jok had a bull called Mijok with
> widespread horns. In the morning, when the cattle were
> released, Longar brought his bull, Mangar. Mijok of Jok
> was still in the cattle-byre. When Mangar came to the
> door of the cattle-byre, Jok told his bull, "Mijok, wake
> up; there is a fight." Mijok got up. They met in front of
> the cattle-byre. While Mijok had part of his body still in
> the byre, he gored Longar's Mangar and killed him. This
> is how Jok got his renowned chant, "Jok who wins his
> fights with his body inside the byre." Then Longar said
> to Jok, "Son of my father, if your bull has killed my bull,
> I have surrendered."

When I asked Bulabek whether this suggested that Jok's
seniority to Longar had been in question prior to this confrontation, he said:

> Jok had always been the senior. Jok was the leader of
> all the people. Longar was a chief, but junior to Jok.

Jok and Longar were the people who had been given the sacrificial meat. Longar took the remaining meat and Jok took the main meat from the sacrificial animal. Jok carried the upper shoulders all night. He carried the upper body of the animal and left the thighs for Longar.

According to the versions collected by Dr. Lienhardt, it is Longar who sacrifices a bull and divides the meat among the families of the leading men who had subdued him in the river. In the version of Giirdit, Longar gave his family the thigh-bone which is now a sacred object for their clan.

The anomaly of Longar or his descendants later sending for Jok's descendant long after the matter of leadership would seem to have been settled is explained by Bulabek, "Chieftainship was contested. And leadership identified itself from the very beginning as being between Longar and Jok. That is where it first appeared. Later, the son of Longar again said he would lead the people, but when leadership became difficult for him, he sent for the son of Jok."

Chief Pagwot Deng's comments on the myth of Pajok leadership—being himself from the Dhiendior—are less ambivalent about the relative position of Jok and Longar, for he asserts that it was their ancestor Longar who was first the paramount leader, but admits that leadership became too formidable for him and was therefore handed over to Jok.

When we came from the Byre of Creation, it is we who led the way of the black people. Our clan, Dhiendior, first led the Dinka, but along the way our leadership was spoiled. So the tribe gave your ancestor, Jok, the leadership and we remained behind, we the Dhiendior. All this talk of competition for power, it is the government which brought all that. When the country was spoiled, the chief of our clan, Dhiendior, left the tribe. It was your grandfather who collected the people, you see.

The second Ngok interview did not include any members of

Dhiendior or Pajok, except myself. The bias of those interviewed was unequivocally for Pajok's preeminence, even though the paradox of Longar initially having been the leader continued to be mentioned. According to Chol Adija:

> When men were created, Jok was the first to come out. It was he who broke the way through the Tree of Creation and came out first. And when he came out, he remained behind while Longar led the way. He said, "Longar, you go to the front."
> Longar went ahead. But the world confounded him. So Jok was fetched.

In answer to my question as to whether Longar had initially been superior to Jok, Chol Adija said:

> He claimed that he was greater than Jok. But then his own eyes saw and he surrendered. When the way of the people became blocked and they could not proceed, it was because the country had become too formidable for him. When a large river confronted the people, a river as large as the river of Khartoum, there was nowhere for people to cross. When Jok came, he decorated Acai and sacrificed her into the river and the river dried up.

Longar's initial seniority becomes more apparent in the words of Acueng Deng. After presenting the theme of Jok emerging from the Tree of Creation with his sacred spears and Longar assuming the lead but failing to make the people cross the river, Acueng describes the scene:

> When people came to a standstill, Jok was called to the front. He came and said, "What is the matter? Longar, what has stopped the people of my father?" Longar said, "The earth has baffled me. There is nowhere to cross." Jok said, "And what will become of the people then?" Longar said, "It is for you to see!" Jok said, "Very well; then go to the back; you go to the back; you have be-

come a junior son. I will let the people of my father cross; you will see with your own eyes."

Jok's words evidently show that he considered being in the front as conferring a higher status than being in the back where, according to the earlier version, he was supposed to perform the more vital function of protecting the people. That he was willing to go to the front and leave the back further supports the contention that the claim of his protecting the people from the back was more a rationalization after the fact of his eventual supremacy in order to give such supremacy original roots.

When I asked whether Jok and Longar were related, Acueng simply answered in the affirmative, while Loth gave a more elusive answer by saying "People originally emerged as one family." And according to his half-brother, Chol, "People were one; they were all related."

Acueng continued with a vivid description of the miracle in the water:

Jok said, "I will let them cross."

"Well," said Longar, "I shall watch to see where you will let them cross." Jok then took his daughter and called all his people, "All those with copper bracelets, give them to me." He collected copper bracelets, and bracelets, and bracelets. Then he decorated the girl. People said, "Jok, what do you intend to do with a live human being?"

He said, "She alone? Is she equal to this entire people of my grandfather? I shall offer her to the river so that the people can cross. She is the canoe in which the people will paddle across."

People protested: some were forcefully constrained from stopping the girl; some were doing other things; all were trying to save the child. They said the child should be spared. But Jok proceeded ahead with the child. He took her into the river and as he was walking deeper and deeper, he was singing hymns and praying. As he walked, the river behind him dried up and continued to dry up. By the time he reached the center of the river, the child was taken from him by the powers of the river and submerged under the water. She was taken from him by the people of the river. She was snatched from him as he sang hymns and prayed, going deeper and deeper into the river. Suddenly, as she disappeared, the whole river went down and dried up. Then the people followed him and he continued to lead them holding his spears, the same spears which are still licked today on oath-taking. He continued to lead, singing hymns and holding his spears until he crossed to the other side.

The people followed him until they crossed to the other side. After they crossed, they did not stop; they continued to walk on. Some went that way, others branched this way, and yet others branched that way. Some remained there and others remained in other places. They then became known as tribe so and so and tribe so and so. The Twic went that way, the Rek went that way, and others went other ways. But it was he, this one Jok, who led all the peoples. That is why, whenever he had a quarrel with any of the peoples he had left behind, the Twic, the Rek, and others, he could destroy their country with his spiritual power.

The mentions of a man on the saddle in the version given by Bulabek Malith, and of the people in the river who took the girl from Jok according to the version given by Acueng Deng, presumably refer to early contact with foreigners who might have been horse-riders. I have heard of both the saddle and the people in the river in versions not included in this volume. On several occasions I have also heard that the people to whom Acai was sacrificed were white. They are envisioned as "real white," implying that they were not human beings but spirits. However, that might simply have been an exaggeration of what must then have been still an unfamiliar color of the skin on the Europeans or Arabs. The myth also indicates earlier origins to the practice of giving children into slavery to save individuals or whole populations, which we know to have been practiced during the nineteenth-century upheavals.

The argument that the river spirits or "supernatural people," to whom Acai was sacrificed, presumably into slavery, were in fact ordinary people, but strangers, is substantiated in the account given by Loth Adija.

> When Longar was in the lead, he came to a wide river. It was such a big river people did not know how to cross. The people who were in the river said, "You cannot cross." People were afraid. So Longar returned and said to Jok, "The way is blocked. And this is treeless land where people cannot settle."
>
> Jok said, "How has the way ended?"
>
> Longar said, "The river is full and when people approach, there are people in the river who say, 'If you come, we will kill you in the river.'"
>
> So Jok said, "I will go and look into that."
>
> Then he went. And when he arrived, the people in the river reappeared and said, "If you come, you will see!"
>
> Jok said, "What if I give you cattle?"
>
> They said, "We do not want cattle."
>
> "What if I give you sheep and goats?"
>
> They said, "We do not want them."
>
> Then he said, "If you insist, I have only one daughter, but I can still give her to you."
>
> With the mention of the daughter, the river people submerged into the water without saying anything more to Jok.
>
> Jok then returned and said, "You people, we are leaving."

He then took bracelets off people's arms and white beads to decorate his daughter. Then he took her into the river as he sang hymns. He was also carrying his sacred spears pointed to the back [to indicate peacefulness]. He was holding his daughter's arm. And then he walked further and further into the water. His daughter was by his side. And when they reached the deepest point where people would normally drown, the girl was pulled down. The water then separated; one part ran that way and another part ran that way and the people crossed. That is how the Dinka came to this side of the river into this land.

Loth Adija then turns to the second strand of the myth of Longar's competition with Jok through their bulls, stressing Longar's obstreperousness and provocativeness, which are unbecoming of a chief, as contrasted with Jok's chiefly qualities. Both these attributes are seen as reflected in the characters of the bulls, a fact which can only be fully appreciated by knowing the extent to which the Dinka identify a man's personality with a bull, including his designation by the bull's name or metaphoric title.

[Jok's] bull behaved like a chief so that he did not mix with cattle; he would graze and go back into the cattle-byre. Longar's bull had subdued all the bulls in the herds, except Mijok. Longar said, "I am driving him to that bull in the byre which people consider the chief. This chieftainship which we are disputing, we shall settle with our bulls." So he drove the bull toward the cattle-byre. Mangar advanced toward the byre. Mijok looked out and bellowed. Jok then said, "Mijok, here is a deadly beast which has been killing the bulls; he is being driven to you. He is coming to kill you." As Mijok heard that, he ran to the door of the byre and extended his front quarters outside the byre while his hind quarters remained inside. Then he waited. Mangar advanced. They no longer had

time to work up their anger. They met thus. Mijok quick-
ly pierced through the bladed horn and hit the nape of
Mangar's neck. Mangar fell in a heap in front of the byre.
Thus he died.

Longar said, "What has he done?"

The people said, "He has put him to an instant death."

That is how the saying came, "The bull of Jok wins his
wars with part of his body inside the byre; Mijok of the
son of God."

Longar then surrenders in words which are significant as
they reflect what the Ngok see as a unique attribute of Pajok's chieftainship, namely, that they possess two spears, the
smooth unbarbed fishing spear, *lal,* and the bladed fighting
spear, *tong.* According to Loth, Longar said:

> Why Jok has completely defeated me with his power is
> what God gave him from the time of creation. It is em-
> bodied in the bladed spear which he has in addition to
> his rounded spear. If it were the rounded spear alone, I
> too have my rounded spear. Why he defeats me is because
> I do not have a bladed spear. I have tried all people and
> no one has defeated me. And why he is the only one
> who defeats me, I cannot understand. Perhaps it is be-
> cause he is so quiet and it is I who offend him. I shall
> leave him to lead.

In the view of Loth, "Only the Pajok have the two sacred
spears. All the other divine leaders have only the fishing
spear. None of them has the bladed spear." As we know from
Giirdit's version of the Longar myth to Lienhardt, Longar
"spat on an *alal* spear and a war-spear and gave them to
Agoth."[16] The Ngok claim to the uniqueness of their chieftainship in this respect is therefore another illustration of the
general Dinka orientation of historical facts to the limited
world they know and in promotion of their local interests.

16. Lienhardt, *Divinity and Experience,* p. 176.

In view of the near-universal acceptance of Longar as the supreme authority who even when outwitted by other leaders merely confers on them some of his own authority rather than be subordinated to his subduers, the Ngok strand of the myth must be deemed to be a reflection of the historical realities which mark the evolution of greater centralization and chiefly authority among the Ngok, under the paramount leadership of the Pajok, than has been the case elsewhere in Dinkaland where the systems remained "ascophalous," or autonomous along the lines of the lineage segmentation system, until quite recently. As I have already said, evidence of the Pajok dominance and their protective role under the nineteenth-century conditions of contact with the outside world is more appropriate for later sections. It is, however, worth stressing the Ngok's conviction about the predominance of the Pajok not only among the Ngok but indeed among all the Dinka. Whenever I asked the Ngok chiefs and elders whom I interviewed as to the group identity of the people Jok led, the answer was invariably, "All the black peoples." Indeed, when Loth Adija found himself speaking of the Ngok in the context of Longar's eventual surrender, Chol Adija retorted, "It was not the Ngok; it was all the black peoples." Loth withdrew with an explanation, "Yes, it was all the black peoples. It is just that our mouths are more used to the name Ngok."

According to Acueng Deng:

> All this black world did not know any other chieftainship besides the chieftainship of Jok. People looked to the Ngok for chieftainship. Ngok chiefs would give even a ring to a person and send him to another tribe saying, "Take this man and place him at your head; he will be your chief and you should listen to his words." The only people whose chieftainship you [Pajok] are not in are the family of Bilkuei. They found it later by themselves as a leadership of God—they used to cure smallpox. As for

the chieftainship by which a person controls a tribe and whereby a lineage is said to provide chiefs, it was all sought from you. You gave authority to people who would then call their people and take a small ring which the Great Chief in Ngokland would bless but only with a small spit, not with much spit [lest they pass their own power away] . . . .

Chieftainship then spread to other tribes one by one. All these people came here for their chieftainship. All the people who have now flourished got theirs from here. Then each man went and learned.

Whatever the particular historical justification for the claims of the Ngok to the original leadership of not only all the Dinka but the black world as they know it—and the accounts of the Southern chiefs also provide abundant evidence for the preeminent role of Ngok leadership with respect to all the Dinka—the versions of the Ngok clearly reflect the general bias the Dinka display in recounting their history. While a certain element of conviction marks the partial way with which a Dinka recounts myths, all Dinka are aware of the fact that people tend to distort history to enhance their image and therefore promote their influence in contemporary society. This is why, with the exception of the few undisputed leaders, the Dinka would tend to avoid recounting the myths of his lineage in front of a possible competitor who might take offense at any incidental distortions or, as the Dinka see it, at the bitter truth that his lineage is subordinate. Such myths of leadership and contemporary claims to influence on account of them are usually verbalized in songs only, but then lavishly. Of course, a Dinka will give a partial account of a myth to an outsider, as many did to Godfrey Lienhardt, because they are aware of his impartiality, provided the company does not involve Dinka members of a competitive group.

One of the proliferating complications is that, whereas

primogeniture has generally been the rule in Dinka chieftainship, there have been so many intervening disruptions that
have brought an end to the leadership of chiefly lineages in
many tribes. This is what Chief Albino Akot meant when he
said, "The people who were originally known for chieftainship have been reduced." But that in itself does not vanquish
other people's claims to original leadership, for, even when
chieftainship is newly acquired, the Dinka often tend to
reconstruct its roots in such a way as to ultimately link it to
original sources, thereby enhancing its divine authority. It
is this value which Chief Biong Mijak was emphasizing with
respect to the Pajok when he said, "Our people came from
the Byre of Creation," implying an unbroken line of chiefs.
According to Loth Adija, also speaking in comparative terms
to emphasize the importance of permitting the chieftainship
of Pajok to continue, contrary to the trend in favor of abol-
ishing chieftainship:

> You see, as we now relate the affairs of the past, the
> chieftainship you hear of in other tribes consists of three
> generations, two generations, three generations, and a
> chieftainship which has lasted long consists of four
> generations or five generations. As for the chieftainship
> of your ancestors, you have been told that it began with
> Jok Athurkok. You know it; you must have heard it from
> your father. It came in that successive line; none of the
> generations in the line has ever been without chieftain-
> ship—not for a single day.

Thon Wai's reference to William Deng Nhial, the Southern
nationalist leader who was assassinated during the civil war,
as "Son of Chief" is also revealing, as it is common knowledge that William Deng was not a son of a chief. This designation implies the Dinka expectation that only a chief's son
becomes a leader and when the facts are otherwise, a chiefly
background tends to be fictionally constructed.

Accounts of chiefs indicate that chieftainship began to spread through the process of segmentation for which the Nilotes are known. As a pastoral people, who have been continuously in search of better pastures, the Dinka spread over a vast territory. Linked with this was the natural increase in their population, necessitating wider land for habitation, especially because much of Dinkaland is often flooded during the wet season. As the higher lands become scarce, groups are sometimes forced to break up in search of dry spots.

From the point of view of leadership, a primary factor has been political dissension, leading to the breakaway of factions of the tribe under the leadership of members of the chiefly lineages who then founded new tribes. Whatever the process, fragmentation and segmentation gave a dynamic character to Dinka leadership. Also mentioned by a number of chiefs was the element of intermarriage. According to Lino Aguer, "All the Dinka know one fact, that man came out as one person and as one people. Then they divided and married and intermarried. They broke up in this process of intermarriage." And in the words of Chief Albino Akot, "Originally, chieftainship was reserved for certain sections. After people of different sections intermarried, chieftainship spread to every section." Also important in this connection are the rules of exogamy, which forbid marriages within a wide circle of relatives and encourage intermarriage from distant circles. The concomitant spread of chieftainship also implies a spread of claims to chieftainship and a sense of social and political equality. But while many changes have taken place in this process, there has been a basic continuity in the fundamental concepts of the Dinka about class and leadership structure as well as in the principle of primogeniture, even though the facts of a particular case usually permit a flexible interpretation and application of the rules.

It is only very recently that a certain pride in an independent acquisition of power has begun to emerge. The attitude of the older generation of chiefs on this innovation is quite unequivocal, as the words of Chief Arol Kacwol show.

> I and my sub-chiefs are vexed because our country is spoiling; the question of two chiefs is spoiling our country; when a man called Malual Arob, who had helped the Sudan for so long, died, his chieftainship was taken away and given to somebody we do not even know. Another man called Maker Gum served the government for very long. When he died, his people broke away and his things have now become the things of other people. These are the things that will spoil our country.

Indeed, even Chief Yusuf Deng, who takes pride in the fact that he was chosen by his people from a non-chiefly background, finds the modern method of election contrary to the dignity of chieftainship.

> A new way of selecting chiefs is coming. . . . Some men now run after the people and talk to them trying to persuade them to accept them as chiefs. This is not the way chieftainship was in the past. In the past, a man was selected by his people because they saw him as the right man to be the chief. A man did not go about asking for votes as they do now in elections. This is not the way the Dinka selected their chiefs. When they selected their chiefs, it was not that a clan declared itself to be chiefs; the clan was designated to provide chiefs. Elders came from different sections of the tribe and they said, "So and so is the man we have accepted to be our chief; he is the one who will run our country well and it is he who will take care of our children. That was how it was. But if it is a chieftainship for which one gets up and goes and talks to people in the tribe and says, "I am the chief," then I think that kind of chieftainship will not do the job.

As is quite evident in the foregoing accounts, a recurrent theme in Dinka mythology is the importance the Dinka have attached to leadership throughout their known history and particularly during critical periods. In the words of Chief Giirdit:

> All this talk—you son of Deng, there were great men who were keeping this country. There was your grandfather, Kwol Arob, the son of Arob Biong; there were people like Allor Ajing; there were people like Bol Nyuol and people like Chom in Twicland; and in Apuk, there was Thiik. They were the people who would go and meet with your grandfather. There were also people like Yor Maker and people like Mawien Arik and . . . Kwol. And it was the big things of the country and how they would run their country that they would meet and talk about; such things as how people should relate to each other on the borders. Those were the ways of those big leaders of the past. And what is now said, that there is this and that, is all a lie. There was chieftainship in the past. Chieftainship is not a new thing. . . . Chieftainship is an ancient thing; it is not a thing of today. A country is lived in because of a chief.

Chief Arol Kacwol, reacting to the anthropological assertion that the Dinka are among the chiefless peoples where force was the deterrent behind order, said:

> It is true, there was force. People killed one another and those who could defeat people in battle were avoided in respect. But people lived by the way God had given them. There were the Chiefs of the Spear. If anything went wrong, they would come to stop the people from fighting. Each side would tell the chief its cause and he would go to each side and settle the matter without blood. Men of the spear were against bloodshed. That was the way

God wanted it from the ancient past when he created
people. . . .
    People would say to themselves, "This man, if he says
something, it should be respected. No one should go beyond his words."

When I told Chol Adija about the anthropological assertion
of the chiefless nature of traditional Dinka society, and how
these theories were based on information collected from
fieldwork among the Dinka of Chief Giirdit, he remarked
almost angrily:

Oh! Did I not go back to the roots of chieftainship
before? I said chieftainship began with Jok. He emerged
with it and with his bladed spear and rounded spear. This
is a chieftainship which came from the Byre of Creation.
All the black peoples, no people do not know Allor; no
people do not know Biong; no people do not know Arob.
It is a lie that people like Giirdit said. People like Giir
emerged more recently on the Kir.

Nor can it be said that the institution the chiefs are describing is the creation of colonial powers, for, as they themselves
say, colonial invasions on the whole brought disaster which
had to be confronted by the chiefs in defense of their people.
In some areas, traditional chiefs were eliminated in the confrontation. Commenting on the Mahdist period, for instance,
Robert Collins writes that "One must regard the Mahdist
invasion as extended raids which upset the traditional pattern
of the tribal life and left nothing behind but anarchy and fear.
Many of the tribal leaders were killed or carried off with
their tribesmen in captivity."[17]
    It is indeed likely that what anthropologists found during
the colonial era is the remnant of the disruptive anarchy

17. Robert Collins, *The Southern Sudan: 1883–1898* (New Haven, Yale University Press, 1962), p. 177.

imposed by outside aggression. Chief Giirdit commented on the predicament which then faced the usually helpless chiefs.

Where could the chiefs find their strength? They had no power. Only those who managed to establish some relationship with the Turks became the point of refuge for the Dinka. It was through those people that the Dinka found some peace. And even the fact that there are Dinka today—people are here because of your family. It was your great-grandfather and your grandfather who saved the people. It was they who saved the people. Many sections have disappeared. Some have gone into slavery. In some sections only thirty or forty remained. A section with fifty people was considered a large one. You people have not witnessed any destruction. Even the war which has been going on between the South and the North is not destruction. The earlier destruction was one in which people slept in the forest. It was a destruction in which, if you saw a man, you considered yourself dead—any man at all, even a black man, if you saw him, you were dead if you had no greater strength of your own. And he would take your things.

The importance of chieftainship goes back to the very essence of the fundamental values of the Dinka. We have already seen the value of immortality through posterity, its familial orientation, and its religious implications. We have also seen the interconnections between notions of God and Fatherhood within this conceptual framework. To the Dinka, a tribe and a country are conceptualized as extended families. This is indeed expressed in the terminology used for designating both the country and the tribe. *Baai,* the word used for these organizational concepts, may also mean home or family.

The relationship status of the leader, like that of the family head, vis-à-vis God and his human dependents, is that of the senior son of God and the eldest brother or father to his family members or followers. As a father is considered a divine leader, so is the leader of a tribe or a country, with even greater spiritual powers commensurate to his larger community obligations. Dr. Lienhardt analyzed this divine familial complex in the following words:

> The Dinka sometimes speak of their prototypical master of the fishing spear and culture-hero . . . as "the eldest son" of Divinity. As such he shares something more of the "father's" nature than do other men, and is for that reason a point at which men and Divinity meet. . . . He represents men to the divine; he mediates the divine to men. This mediation of Dinka spearmasters and prophets, made possible by a combination analogous to that in the eldest son of the dual roles of son and father, is one of the most important concomitants, for Dinka social structure, of the attribution of transcendent fatherhood to divinity.[18]

It is however such anthropological emphasis on the divine authority of Nilotic leaders and on the democratic spirit of the Nilotic individual which has led to a theoretical de-emphasis on the secular aspect of their chieftainship and on the importance of the institution of chieftainship itself. This has partly been an interpretational outcome but it has also been the result of anthropological bias in favor of the spiritual aspect and idealized freedom of the Nilotics from the restraints of law and government. This dualist attitude of anthropoligists is lucidly expressed by Professor Lucy Mair's description of the traditional authority of Dinka chiefs in these normatively somewhat ambiguous words:

> Some of them were regarded with great respect, and

18. Lienhardt, *Divinity and Experience,* p. 45.

they were described in ideal terms as if they were rulers who commanded obedience. But one has to take such description with some skepticism because, in a world as wicked as the one we live in, it is rarely possible to command obedience without commanding force.[19]

Dr. Lienhardt maintains that he has "heard it said of a renowned master of the fishing spear of the past that he led (*kwath,* the word for driving cattle) his people, and ordered (*cieng*)—'ruled' would be too strong a word to use of anyone among the Dinka—the whole country."[20] To the Dinka, speaking of "driving" the people in the manner of cattle, which is now used to describe police escort of offenders, is as indicative of external control, if not more so, as the terms *dom* (hold), *mac* (tether) or *muk* (keep, control, or maintain), which are often used to describe the leader's control and authority over his people. Leading, in the sense Lienhardt prefers, is best expressed by the expression *wat nhom,* literally "leading the head" or *wat nhiim* to indicate plural for the led. This expression is also often used to describe the leadership functions of the chiefs and connotes more than guidance, as it also implies positive obligations for the general welfare of the led. It is true that all these terms conceptually relate to cattle, but that is because the significance of cattle permeates Dinka social structure and cattle terminology is largely used for designating such structural descent and/or territorial organizations.

To emphasize his point, Godfrey Lienhardt avoided the use of the term "chief," preferring instead the expression "master of the fishing spear." When Evans-Pritchard and Paul Howell decided to use the term "chief," they saw to it that it was qualified as "The Leopard Skin Chief." All of them agreed that the Nuer and the Dinka lacked law as they lacked any central legislature and authority to enforce law.

19. Lucy Mair, *Primitive Government* (Baltimore, Penguin Books, 1962), p. 48.
20. Lienhardt, "Western Dinka," p. 48.

The main concern of the anthropologists, as it seems to me and as I have already indicated, was to demonstrate the positives of democracy and self-discipline implicit in the existence of order despite lack of controlling authority or government. Hence the paradoxical view of Evans-Pritchard about the Nuer system as "ordered anarchy." It was to demonstrate the interrelationship of authority and control in Nilotic society with the spiritual and moral values of the people that led these anthropologists to give so much emphasis to the religious component of leadership. The chief among the Nilotics was not a corporal authority whose power rested on his potential to impose physical sanctions on the culprit; he was "the father" of his people, the representative of God and ancestors and other mythical participants. As such, he carried the all-embracing responsibility for the welfare of man living in society. He had to regulate the forces of nature through his divine powers so that the total cosmology would be in accord and factors that might lead to natural disaster be controlled. The availability of fish in the rivers, the supply of rainfall, the control of grain-eating birds and insects, the fertility of the land and the well-being of the people and their livestock were all within his authority. If fish were in short supply, if there was too much rain, if river and lagoons were flooded, if birds and insects destroyed the crops, if the cosmological discord brought disease and animal attacks, it was for him to atone for whatever wrong had brought the discord and reestablish the prerequisite harmony for well-being through prayer and sacrifice. His mediation between individuals and groups, using largely persuasive strategies, was a feature of this all-embracing responsibility toward the dual worlds of man and spirits, but in terms of political and governmental power, not less significant. As Chief Yusuf Deng pointed out, the power of words is mightier than the power of the arm. But the Dinka must not be understood to rely purely on persuasion for, in the ultimate resort, there is the deep-rooted expectation that contravening the chief's words invokes the sanction of his spiritual powers which may inflict a curse and perhaps death on an uncooperative culprit. Indeed, it is this ultimate power to curse and inflict physical punishment on the wrongdoer which is symbolized by the sacred spears which, though ritual objects of invocation, represent weapons of great destruction for the Dinka. These two elements of the chief's functions are brought together in times of war against outside aggression. He is then expected to pray for victory and ritually point his spears at the enemy, willing the enemy's destruction. According to Acueng Deng:

> These spears enable us to see the people with whom we fight, but they cannot see us. We can literally pierce them with our spears and destroy them until we ourselves give up the fight. In the olden days of our elders, they would literally pierce the enemies with their spears and stain their hands with the blood of their victims. The spears would be plastered to the hands of the warriors by the blood of the victims.

As incidents during the recent civil war demonstrated, so dependent on the chief are the Dinka that to kill their leader, as happened in a number of areas, including Bor and the Ngok, is to "spoil" their world beyond doubt. This theme comes across quite vividly in a number of Dinka folktales in which human beings are depicted as destroying lion camps merely by killing the lion chief. All his subjects subsequently disperse aimlessly and individually, not caring even for friends or relatives for, as they are often heard to argue, "Why care about anyone in a world in which the chief is killed?"

The importance, indeed the indispensability, of chieftainship in the minds of the Dinka was recently illustrated by a story I heard repeated in many circles and cited in one of the interviews from the Ngok. According to the story, there was a cattle-camp without a chief. One day, a tame lion came disguised as a man and wanted to know who the chief was. He was told that there was no chief and that the people of the camp wanted total freedom from any authority. He advised them to look for a son of a chief and make him their chief, for without a chief their camp was completely unprotected and could be destroyed even by one lion. They refused. He went and then returned as a lion to attack the camp. He destroyed the camp and left unrecognized. Then he returned again as the human being they had met. He wanted to know what had happened to the camp and was told of the destruction by the lion. Then he recalled his advice to them adding that if they had had a chief, that chief would have found some means of controlling the lion or appeasing him in some way to avoid destruction. His advice was subsequently followed and the camp found itself a son of a chief to be their chief.

So vital to public order and to the physical well-being of man in living society is divine chieftainship that, traditionally, the chief was not permitted to die a natural death. When he was so ill that death was thought imminent or so old that he lost his physical and mental vitality and was at the brink of death, he was buried alive. Quite often, he himself would take the initiative by making his dying will and requesting to be buried. This is a debated point among anthropologists. Some believe that it was merely mythological, but the Dinka believe that the practice existed until it was abolished by the British administration.

Even under the circumstances of change which the Dinka have undergone, the chiefs have led the way, for it is the chief that must first confront the stranger who threatens the stability of his traditional order and it is such outsiders who are ultimately the agents of change. In terms of indulgences, it is also the chief who is likely to enrich himself with the merits of any adventurous ideas or practices in order to promote and maintain his supremacy over his subjects in value-institutional structures. It is only recently, when the radicalism of change has outpaced them, that they have felt threatened by it and may logically oppose it or, if possible, join the bandwagon, as indeed some of the chiefs interviewed seem to be doing.

The sanctity of chieftainship as an institution on which the Dinka have always depended for public order and social welfare derives ultimately from God's will and is only justified by the leader's attributes as the father of his people. In the words of Chief Arol Kacwol, "That was the way God wanted it from the ancient past when he created people." But despite this religious derivation, it is important to bear in mind the broad-based authority of the Dinka chief and the multifaceted responsibility which the Dinka associate with leadership. Even in today's society, this traditional outlook accounts for the respect one sees the Dinka show the authority of modern government, often expressed in songs of praise for their leaders; in turn they expect from the government protection and the improvement of their living conditions.

Migration

One of the fields in which Nilotic studies is very limited is the history of migration. This is more a field for historians than for anthropologists; and oral history as a discipline, the only possible source available, has hardly given any attention to the Nilotics. But another reason for the lack of evidence in this field is the people's own vagueness about their history of migration. In many cases, the chiefs I interviewed simply had no idea about where the Dinka came from. One general assertion is that people came from the east, a direction usually associated with the sun, in turn associated with the source of life. It is thus possible that association is more conceptual than factual.

This account from Chief Lino Aguer is typical of the generalized assertions about the origins of Dinka migration: "We, the Dinka, did not come from the front [the west]. . . . The Dinka came from the back [the east]. They went as far as the places we are now holding. These were the last places we reached. But we began from the east. That is what we heard from our fathers."

Nonetheless, Lino Aguer was next to Giirdit in furnishing details which might appear as a mere reflection of the settlement-situation of the Dinka world today, but also have aspects which display some intimate knowledge of the origin of these realities. To quote more from him:

> People went up to Kosti and people went up to Khartoum. When the Dinka found the land dry and sandy, a ground of no use because he was a man with cattle, that's where he turned downward. He went up to Baar Ajak. He came and found a place of water and a place of grass. So they divided. Some went forward and some stayed behind and others were in the center, like the Rek.
>
> But the way we heard about the migration of the Dinka, they left from the river there, from the east, and went to the land of the Arabs and then turned back to Rekland. That is how the Dinka came.
>
> The Twic passed through Luacland. There is today a place called the Shrine of the Twic between the Rek and Agar, between Luac and Agar of Wol. They hit Luac and then came out of Luac and turned inside again up to Nuer. When they found at Kosti that the Dinka of the North were coming back because the land was dry, they came back with them to Baar Ajak; Baar Ajak belongs to River Lol. They first found the River Kir and then the River Lol. They divided with the Rek in Luacland. Rek went and crossed the river at Meshra and the Twic went to the land they are now occupying. That is the story of Dinka migration.

Chief Giirdit was exceptional in displaying impressive knowledge of details about the migration of certain tribes of the Dinka including the names of specific places they passed through or settled in, and some of the social and interpersonal situations involved. Yet, even in the accounts of Giirdit, one senses a dogmatic belief in his knowledge of the truth, curiously combined with a flexible recreation of occurrences to meet some desired end in a contemporary situation.

People did not come from above. People came searching for land. The land they came from, did you not find it in your travels? It's not a land that could sustain life. So they crossed territories. They came crossing the lands in search of a good land. They went as far as Bor and then returned. And as for your people, there is a cattle-camp in our territory called Makuany Ngok where they first settled and then left. The people called Twic did not pass through this territory. The Twic passed through Nuerland. I don't know whether the people called Luac are your people. They are a single people here, but they have their roots among the Nuer. You came across the territory and went ahead, leaving a branch of your tribe called Ngok behind. You first came through the land of Agar, through which all the Dinka passed. . . .

The Ngok came and passed through the country of Awan Parek. Then they crossed under the Ruweng and hit a place called Pawic. Then they continued and hit Makuac, the place we now call Makuac of Ngok. They came and crossed into the Toc. . . .

They crossed and then turned around and went ahead to the northern part of our Toc. They crossed it and hit the land of Gier, then came around again and crossed the Kir River, and went into the land they now inhabit. The Twic came after them, as far as the place called Marial Baai—that Marial of ours called Marial of Aguok.

They were the first to reach there. When our group came, they crossed by way of Luac and then parted. One group became Apuk Padek. They crossed to the other side and remarked, "Here we have found the beginning of a good *toc*." They settled on that *toc*. So we said they should be called Padooc because they had blessed themselves. The other Apuk passed that way and went and found a small *toc* near the river. There they found a lot of hippos in the river: so we said we could call them the Jur of the River [Jurwir]. Then we came that way, crossing the country until we came to a place called Lou. There we lived, but later it didn't satisfy us so we left. We came up to the borders, then turned around to a different land which we found to have more grass. In that territory, during the dry season we heard the bellows of a bull. He was a brown bull. Some people said, "Is there a cattle-camp here?" Others said, "No, there can't be a cattle-camp. How can a bull bellow at night? If it were a cattle-camp, the bulls would bellow in the morning." So people went to see. They found a fire. It was a cattle-camp.

It was the camp of the people called Lueel, the people who built the mounds now in Dinkaland. After a fight the Lueel were chased away, but later returned and said, "What people are you?"

They said, "We are the Apuk."

He said, "So you are called the Apuk?"

They said, "Yes."

"Very well," the man said. You will now be known as the Pathuot. I am called Thuot and my tribe is also known as Thuot. You will be the Pathuot."

Then they left. But the Twic also went and sent them away from their new settlement. Then the Aguok and the Apuk fought. Apuk chased the Aguok to a place called "Pinydit" [The Great Land]. It was called "The Great

Land" because one of the Aguok said, "O people, even if the Apuk have chased us away from our land, this too is a great country. And if we settle in it, it will also prove to be a land for settlement." And so they said, "We might as well spend the summer here."

The Malual passed by way of Alal. They hit the Alal called Bar. They followed it until they reached Kongder. It was called Kongder—"reach first"—because it was the first place to be reached. They were with my grandfather who said that this place will be called Kongder. Then they continued to a place called Paliet, the land of Aguok. They said this will be called Paliet because people have become like beggars. They went until they hit Ajak. And when people went, they brought *thou* [the heglig fruit] and *ajuet* [another fruit] as contributions to the chief. They are the Mading Aweil. Then they went and when they reached Kuang Ayat, they came to a dead end. They found a Jur tribe called Chad and a brown Jur [Jur Mathiang], who stopped them from going further. And people were going on in the hope that there would be something good ahead. But they did not find anything good.

As is already apparent in the foregoing accounts, Dinka versions of their source-country always imply that they had once settled further north in less grassy areas, and some even mention names of northern areas they are supposed to have once inhabited. One Ngok version by Bulabek Malith mentions the area of Sennar.

Sennar is said to be the place where a bull came from. The clan which owned that bull is still in our Ngokland, a clan called Bong. The bull of Bong left Jebel Moya and crossed the Ngol. He would go and spend the dry season on the Ngol, eating the grass that sprouted after the dry grass was burnt. The owner of the bull said,

"Why does the bull go during the dry season and come back during the wet season? I am going to follow him to find out where he goes." So he followed the bull and found Ngol. That is how our people left and went to Ngol.

Chief Ayeny Aleu, displaying a skepticism toward Dinka myths about where man was created, presented his own thoughts about the place of creation and mentioned Shendi, north of Khartoum, as the place the Dinka later migrated from.

There are such lies said, for instance, that in a place called Akorcok people walk on their knees and hands. It is said people emerged from the waters crawling on their knees and hands. It is said that that is where our people crawled out of the water. But in my thinking, it seems that people were created somewhere else and then they came and found a river which they crossed. It was later at Shendi that people came crawling out of the waters. It is Shendi where people actually emerged from the water. But people were created somewhere else.

The vividness with which the Dinka reconstruct certain situations from their past, and the endless variations in the details they attribute to those situations, illustrate the creativity associated with memory. In reality, the Dinka are less interested in the factual details, and far less in the apparent logic of those details and facts, than they are in their theoretical value and its relevance to current objectives. Migration tends to be associated with the search for better grazing land or separations resulting from interpersonal or intergroup feuds.

Implicit in their explanation of migration as a search for grass is a kind of self-justification and exaltation of their present land as the best. As we have already seen, many observers have written of Dinka pride in their country and their despising of other people's lands as inferior to their own.

Indeed, before modern education and the post-colonial labor situation resulted in a mass exodus into urban centers, the Dinka used to regard any migration outside their tribes, however temporary, as despicable, and it was often deprecated in slanderous songs. Even today, young men and women who migrate for labor into urban centers will find it necessary to justify it in songs, usually as a search for cash to acquire cattle. That the Dinka justify their migration in terms of a search for land and regard their country as the best is very apparent in Giirdit's remarks in the passage quoted earlier: "The land they came from, did you not find it in your travels? It's not a land that could sustain life."

Once the overall justification is made, the name of the country from which they migrated does not really matter to the Dinka. This dismissal of the past abode is rather paradoxical in view of their attachment to, and pride in, the territory they now live in. One would have assumed that their pride in the fatherland is inherent rather than merely the outcome of the objective assessment of their land value, even though from the point of view of a pastoral life their land is highly suited. Again, partial explanation can perhaps be found in the dynamic nature of tradition which has for long escaped the attention of observers. Despite basic continuity, tradition adapts itself to the existing realities of any given period. Ironically, it is such flexibility which gives tradition the resilience to withstand the forces of change. It is possible to see how the Dinka pride in their past homeland could be transferred to the new haven where circumstances had forced them to settle.

3. Contact with Outsiders

Although Dinka mythology indicates that they must have been in contact with the outside world from time immemorial, they only acknowledge having displaced a people called Lueel, and are particularly conscious of the more recent nineteenth-century contact with three sets of people: Northern Sudanese, Turko-Egyptians, and the British. The impact of these peoples may be classified into the pre-Condominium, the Condominium, and the Independence periods.

Pre-Condominium

As we saw in their stories of migration, the Dinka fought, conquered, and displaced the Lueel who had inhabited the area they now occupy. Apart from the mounds they made on which to build their homes for protection against floods, and which still appear throughout Dinkaland, and the enormous amounts of tiny potsherds which cover the plains near these mounded settlements, testifying to the fact that they must have been skilled potters, hardly anything is known of these mysterious victims of the Dinka. Even the name applied to them is not uniform, for while most Dinkas know them as Lueel, which implies that they were brown, some refer to them as the Girma and some call them the Chad. Although they were pushed out, some of them were assimilated into Dinka tribes. On the whole, the history of Dinka confrontation with them seems so distant or insignificant in Dinka memory that it occupies only a minor part of their mythological history—usually the simple fact of Dinka victory and occupation.

But precisely the opposite was true of Dinka contacts with the stronger and more formidable invaders from the North;

because here they were weaker and suffered, Dinka history and myth about them is richer and uniquely morbid. This is particularly the case vis-à-vis the Turko-Egyptian and the Mahdist invasions.

Although the Turko-Egyptians and the Mahdists invaded the Dinka to spread their administration, and might therefore be distinguished from the ordinary commercial slave-traders, their raids also involved slavery and were in fact indistinguishable from those of ordinary slave-hunters. Indeed, the Dinka conceptually fuse them and associate them with the total destruction of their world.

It is generally accepted that slavery in one form or another has prevailed along the Nile Valley for as long as recorded history. For most of that time, it is also generally accepted that the Negroid tribes in the South have been consistent victims of slave-raids. However, their own determined resistance and natural barriers protected many of the pastoral peoples from any deep penetration by slave-raiders. Consequently, it was not until the Turko-Egyptian government opened the Bahr El-Ghazal and Equatoria provinces and established relatively more security from outside invaders that the trade became well established and assumed large proportions. It was, however, no easy feat for the Turko-Egyptian rule to establish itself in the South, and although the Turko-Egyptians entered the Sudan as far back as 1821, it was not until the 1870s that they could claim any degree of control. In the process of trying to establish itself, the Turko-Egyptian government carried out punitive expeditions throughout the tribes and, although they encountered strong and determined resistance, the tribes suffered enormously. Chiefs were slain, their people killed, cattle seized, crops taken or burned down and houses destroyed. Under those conditions, it was initially easy for the South to welcome and in places even join the Mahdist revolution against the Turko-Egyptian rule. As I have already mentioned, the

Dinka even adopted and assimilated the concept of the Mahdi into their religion. The great powerful spirit of the sky called Deng was said to have fallen on the Mahdi who then became known to the Dinka as Mahdi, the son of Deng Acuuk—Acuuk, the name for a tiny black ant, being a metaphoric reference to man in relation to God. The Dinka, as well as the rest of the Southern tribes, soon learned that the Mahdists not only had invaded them as the Turko-Egyptians had, with the same objectives of establishing what the tribes saw as outside control, but worse—full-scale slavery returned and intensified. Their resistance was, however, effective, so that Mahdism never succeeded in entrenching itself among most of the Southern tribes.

The experience of the Dinka has been summarized by Major Titherington in the following passage:

> There can be no doubt that their social system and personal outlook, as we so lately found it, was in a state of deterioration directly resulting from the continued harrying they received from the Northern slavers, and the demoralizing effects of half a century of subjection to crime at the hands of every stranger before the coming of the present [British] Government.
>
> That they did not succumb altogether like so many Southern tribes, speaks highly for their stoutheartedness; nor did they take to the vile, but common practice of selling their fellow tribesmen into slavery. They lost hundreds of thousands of cattle; men, women and children in thousands were slaughtered, carried off into slavery, or died of famine; but the survivors kept alive in the deepest swamps, bravely attacked the raiders when they could, and nursed that loathing and contempt for the stranger and all his ways that even now they are just losing.[1]

1. Titherington, "The Riak Dinka," in *Sudan Notes and Records*, 10 (1927).

The Dinka refer to the Turko-Egyptian and the Mahdist periods as the time when the world was spoiled. As is apparent in the interviews, they speak of it with consistency and vividness. And while they tend to fuse these destructive phases, they present the Mahdist revolution as first claiming to rescue the people from the repressions and the exploitation of Turko-Egyptian rule, but then turning out to be itself a major cause of destruction. In the words of Chief Giirdit, "Although the Mahdi started as liberator, his rule became bad. He wanted to enslave the people." Chief Makuei Bilkuei implies that the Dinka first followed the Mahdi as a virtuous leader, but when they discovered the destructiveness of the Mahdist rule, they said to him, "'You are deceiving our people.' And then there was a fight."

So recurrent is the theme of the world's destruction at the hands of the Turks, the Egyptians, and the Mahdists, that it would be impossible to quote all the relevant passages from the interviews. A representative sample will therefore suffice:

Chief Giirdit specifies the Turks and the Dongolawi, the tribe of the Mahdi, as the source of destruction.

> It was the Dongolawi—the Dongolawi and the Turks. They were the people who spoiled our country. They were the people who captured our people and sold them. They would just go and attack any village and capture people. . . .
>
> When the Turks came attacking people and causing disorder, that's when the expression "Turuk" first began. They did not bring any order, nor did they unite the country. They came from your side attacking and also from the south of us, then went to Malual Dinka country and turned to your side again. They went destroying tribes. They would attack and destroy an area, and when they conquered they would take the people and add them to the army as slaves. And when they conquered the next tribe, they would also add them to their group

and use them to attack the next. If a man had children, one might give them a child or two in the hope that they would spare his life and maybe help him with some means of livelihood. That was the way things were.

Chief Makuei Bilkuei made the same point almost obsessively.

Destruction came with the Mahdi. Mahdi was the man who brought destruction. This destruction went to Jok and it went to Nuer and it went to Beir. Mahdi's people were called the Ansar. It was the Ansar who destroyed the country up to Bor here, killing people. It was Mahdi who destroyed the people. His people called Ansar were the people who came with destruction. That is what is called the spoiling of the world. . . . Yes, he would come with camels and donkeys and mules and guns. . . . That's how he killed people. The place called Kwel and the place called Paweny and all those areas, it was he who destroyed them. He destroyed areas until he reached us here. Then he took the people and sold them. So it was the Ansar who destroyed this country. . . .

The Ansar were the people who turned the country upside down, together with the Mahdi and the Egyptians. If you want the real truth, those were the people who destroyed us. That was the disaster which reached us. They said, *"La Illah, ila Allah, Mohammed Rasul Allah."* That was the way they chanted while they slaughtered and slaughtered and slaughtered. Those were the people who destroyed the country.

Chief Makuei claims not to speak from hearsay, for he himself witnessed the Mahdist invasion: "What I was explaining to you, Mading, were the ancient things about the disaster that our people suffered. I have seen the Ansar and I have seen the destruction that came to our people. I saw the horses of the Ansar."

Chief Stephen Thongkol Anyijong gave a more dispassionate account, starting with the first encounter with foreign government in the Turko-Egyptian rule and continuing into the advent of British rule.

> Then came the government. First it came through the Egyptians. They came together with a people called the Turks. When they came, they used to quarrel with our people. Our forefathers fought with them using spears. They did not like the ways of the Europeans who came. They would go and catch people and say, "Come join us." Otherwise, they enslaved them. Our people refused and said, "This cannot be. These people are taking us into a life which is not ours."
>
> Those people withdrew and then came the people of the Mahdi. They also captured our people and treated them like slaves. That of course was not liked by our people. Some would run into the forest. Our people had great men who were the chiefs controlling the tribes. The government would come and call the chiefs and say, "Chiefs, you'd better come and accept this; there is now a new government in the country." But the government which was saying this was not a government which they liked; it was a government which disgraced our people by making them slaves, a government which would capture the big men of the country and tie their hands and drive them away. Some of them were sold to the Egyptians. That was a thing which confused the heads of our fathers before us. Our people went ahead and fought; they fought until the English came.

Addressing himself to some of the particulars of what the spoiling of the world meant to the Dinka, Chief Giirdit concluded his account with the effect on the livestock—the Dinka symbol of wealth.

All the cattle of the Dinka, the Arab took. He took even

the sheep and goats and the grain at home. People used holes in trees to hide seeds in the hope that in the right season they would try to cultivate again. They would then go and take the grain from the holes in the trees to try to sow the seeds. Those were the Arabs. They took everything away.

Chief Ayeny Aleu assessed the spoiling of the world in the following passage:

> It started as a small thing and it continued to be a big thing to the point where people's wives would be pulled away and put inside another man's house. If you asked, "What is it that takes my wife away from me and puts her into that house?" then you were a dead man. A man's son would be seen and if liked, it would be said, "This child is beautiful; I'll take him." And if you asked, "What is it that takes my child from me and puts him behind that man?" that was a reason for your death. . . . He would take a small child and push his head into the ground and blow it up with a pistol. He would take a child and put him in his big bag on a horse and take him away. Only the bigger ones would he take away; the small ones which would cause problems he would not take; he would just kill them and leave them there. People tried to stop the foreigner by the force of the spear but that did not do much good. Whenever people dispersed into the forest, he would follow and pick them up individually from the forest. He would catch them and take them away with him.

With his secondary school education and political background, Chief Albino Akot saw the destruction in the absence of the rule of law.

> Yes, yes, there was destruction. Yes, there was destruction. In the past, the destruction meant that there was no

rule of law in the country. Without the rule of law, the Arabs would come and say, "We will go to the home of so and so to capture people," without any quarrel. They would come and find people at night and attack them. For instance, at three o'clock at night or at four o'clock while people were sleeping, without any word or any warning, they would burn down the villages. People would wake up in surprise in the middle of the night. The strong would be killed. The weak, like children, would be captured and taken away.

While they give detailed accounts of the suffering they underwent in the hands of those outside aggressors, and may mention robbery and enslavement as the motives of their aggression, the Dinka are rather vague about the causes of hostilities, a fact which underscores their view of the spoiled world, devoid of the normal ethical principles which govern conflicts in ordinary human situations. For instance, in answer to my question as to what provoked the wars, Chief Arol Kacwol said:

The reason for which they fought is not easy to find. It is like you [the educated] when you fought [against the North], you had your own reasons for fighting. Your hearts were dissatisfied with the situation after the English left you with the North as one country. And when you, the educated, felt dissatisfied with things you saw with your own eyes and things you heard with your own ears, was that not the reason for your going into the forest, so that you could fight for your cause in your own way? That was what brought the war that has only recently ended. So, we do not know what the exact reasons of that ancient fighting were.

Chief Ayeny Aleu, after describing some of the horrors the Dinka were subjected to during this period, continued:

And there was nothing that really caused the conflict;

there was no quarrel between the people; there was no cause for the conflict. It's just that when he saw your wife, he wanted to take her; and when he saw your child, he wanted to take the child to be his. It is he who wanted to eat the good things that there were; he would eat the fat part of things and throw you the lean part, the bad food that he did not want to eat. When the Dinka wondered why these things were happening and tried to stop them, that was what brought destruction.

Dinka vagueness about the causes of their wars with the Arabs is ironically evident in the following trifling reason which Loth Adija gave to account for the outbreak of what was a near-universal calamity:

What the elders used to say was that the Arabs were chasing—was it not a giraffe? Marieu, were the Arabs not chasing a giraffe in the area of Alabiath? It was said to be a giraffe which the Arabs had killed. Whether they killed it with a gun or with a horse is the part I do not know. . . .

Yes, that was the giraffe the Dinka ate. They carried the meat to the cattle-camp. The people were then traced and found. The Arabs then returned and began their attack with guns. The Arab would ambush people at night and wake the people up. When the people woke he would say, "I am the bull." Then it would be known that the Arabs had come. They began to attack and destroy the Dinka.

But if the accounts of the chiefs and elders present the Dinka as pathetic victims of unscrupulous human hunters, they also substantiate the theme of Dinka resistance which Major Titherington stressed in the passage quoted earlier. Thus, according to Chief Albino Akot, once the message of an Arab attack was transmitted:

The Dinka would beat the drums of war and say, "We

have to go and attack the Arabs." The scouts would go
ahead to look for where the Arabs were. They would
be followed and followed until they were found by these
scouts. The Arabs would stop and sleep, thinking they
had left the Dinka behind, but the Dinka were following
them. The moment they would settle down, the Dinka
would come and attack them. They would kill them just
as they had killed the Dinka. Some people among them
would be captured and the people who had been captured by the Arabs would be released. That's how it
went.

According to Bulabek Malith, the Arab "would go through
the Toc and Mabil and would kill any people he found in
the forest. Then the Dinka would go and search for him and
attack him at night and kill his people also."
Chief Pagwot Deng goes further to substantiate the relative
balance of power that then characterized Arab-Dinka wars.

The Ngok Dinka and the Arabs both killed one another.
The strength of the Arab came only recently when he
found his horses and his guns. In the past, anyone who
was found with food was robbed. This is how we used to
fight. We killed one another. . . .
    The Arabs destroyed us but we also destroyed them.
They captured our people and we captured their people.
This is why there are some Arabs in Dinkaland today. We
used to capture from one another. His man is with us
and our man is with him.

The theme of mutual enslavement is also generally supported by the evidence of the chiefs and elders. For instance, in
answer to whether the Dinka also enslaved the Arabs, Chief
Giirdit remarked, "Oh, yes. Many of them are around now in
Dinkaland. A great many of the Dinka are descendants of
the Arabs. There are many. Some were captured in battle.
They included women. Others were babies thrown away by

their running parents. Some Dinka would come along, pick them up, and raise them."

While the Dinka also captured Arabs and made them slaves, they strongly reject the assertion that slavery was not only practiced by the Arabs, Egyptians, and European traders, but was a customary practice associated with tribal wars and practiced by all, including the Southern tribes among themselves.

According to Bulabek Malith:

> Mading, the affairs of the Arabs, even if things get written down the way you just said they are written, it is because people are telling lies. If this were so, even you yourself, would you not have known? Your grandfather, Arob Biong, when he used to rescue people from the North—all the black people who had been captured—and release them, would he himself not have many slaves if we were a people who liked slaves? Instead, he would come and rescue the slaves and send word to the Southerners—the Nuer, the Dinka, and others—to ask them to come and identify their own people and take them away. A man would come and say, "This is my man," and he would take him away. Those who remained under the protection of your ancestors are people who did not know their relatives. They were people who were not sought after or not recognized by their relatives. Those were the people who remained among us. But for a black man to take a black man to be his slave has never happened among us, not even in war.
>
> Between us, the Dinka, even if we capture the cattle of the Rek, we return them after the war is over. What we used to do in the past, before the government insisted on captured herds being returned, was to retain the cattle we had captured. Only the cattle would remain with us. But a human being created by God was never made a slave by the black man; it was the Arabs who made them

slaves. . . . Slavery is not known to us . . . To capture
people to be slaves among us is unknown. A person unknown to his relatives is the man who stays among us.
And he is not treated like a slave; he becomes a member
of the family. The treatment I told you about before,
where people are crippled and where people's testicles
are pricked, never happened among the black people. All
these elders know it. So, we do not know this slavery.
The people who know it are these brown people—the
Arabs.

Bulabek Malith thus draws a distinction between those
Southerners who were captured from the Arabs in a war
situation and whom the Dinka freed or adopted and assimilated into their family structure (whatever degree of stigma
might continue to be attached to the status of being a captive
or descendant of a captive), and those whom the Arabs
captured with the distinct motive of enslavement. In another
context, Bulabek addressed himself to the issue of the Arabs
whom the Dinka captured, implying that the Dinka were
forced to capture Arabs and did not in fact treat them as
slaves: "When the Arabs fought with our people and destroyed their country, they captured many people from us
and we too captured from them. But their ways are not like
the ways of our people. Our people did not want slaves. It
was the Arabs who wanted slaves from the Dinka."

Chief Biong Mijak categorically asserted that the institution
of slavery did not exist among the Dinka.

What the Arabs have written down is a lie. . . . Even our
ancestors told us they never captured Arab children. People kill each other in war, face to face, but we do not go
and capture people. . . . We have something God gave us
from the ancient past, from the time our ancestors came
leading the people. War has always occurred but we have
war ethics that came with us from the ancient past. . . .

We never ambush anybody; we kill face to face. It is the Arabs who treat us as slaves and capture us in secrecy.

Chief Pagwot Deng admitted to mutual enslavement, but stressed that the practice existed only between the Dinka and the Arabs.

You asked about the black man, whether black people capture themselves and make themselves slaves of one another. We used to fight with the Twic; we captured cattle among them. You kill during a fight. With the Rek, with the Nuer, with Ruweng, that is the way we always fought. We kill face to face; we do not capture people. When they try to capture our cattle we fight with them. But we and the Arabs have a different law. It is the strong man who captures from the weak and you do whatever you do with your victim, you see. Among ourselves, we the black people, we do not capture people. If there are slaves among us, it is people your great-grandfather took from Khartoum to save them from slavery. People who did not have relatives remained in his home and became his relatives. Those are people who did not have relatives and he became their relative. That is all I want to say.

The magnitude of the bitterness the Dinka feel about the history of slavery is not only in the fact that more recent hostilities with the North are reminiscent of the more distant experience with slavers but also because those earlier experiences were so intensive and pervasive that many of those interviewed could give specific examples pertaining to their own families. Stephen Thongkol's father, with two brothers, were supposedly shot and killed by the Arabs; the father of Chief Arol Kacwol was exchanged from slavery with a sister; the father of Acueng was a rescued slave; and so was the grandfather of Albino Akot. Pagwot Deng and Biong Mijak also gave accounts of more recent encounters with slave-raiders or isolated seizure of children by slavers. As we shall see later, even though the British brought an end to slavery in the Sudan, instances of raids or seizure continued for a considerably long time after the establishment of the Condominium rule.

A theme which has not received sufficient attention in the literature on the nineteenth-century upheavals is the degree to which a number of tragedies contributed to the destruction imposed by outside aggression. Among these were invasions by locusts, famine from crop failure, and an epidemic of smallpox. In the words of Chief Arol Kacwol, "It began with famine. Then came the Arabs killing people. The world was truly spoiled." According to Chief Makuei Bilkuei, the Arabs were "followed by smallpox, then locusts came and destroyed the country. . . . That was what happened. It was the Ansar and the smallpox who finished our people. . . . One day war would come, the next day it would be smallpox and the people would fall." Chief Pagwot Deng reverses the order of events and argues that destruction by the Arabs was in fact aided by the prior suffering and weakening of the Dinka due to smallpox and famine.

> Destruction by the Arabs came later. It was smallpox which first started destruction. It destroyed our people so that people could not cultivate. No cattle remained so that there was no milk to sustain the people. Only fish kept the people alive. People were exterminated by famine; the country was spoilt by famine. When the Arab came, he found the people already destroyed. He came hoping to find some food on the riverside. He would leave from Muglad with his cattle. He did not even have clothes in those days; he used to wear leather like the Dinka. But when destruction first came to our people, it was smallpox.

One of the nineteenth-century hostilities to which observers and especially anthropologists have given attention is the Dinka-Nuer hostility. On the whole, the Dinka consider their wars with the Nuer as more or less an internal affair between kindred tribes. They are rarely mentioned as part of the whole conflict or destruction resulting from outside aggression. They were, however, discussed in Ngok interviews with considerable understanding for the ruthlessness with which the Nuer invaded Dinkaland, despite their alleged eventual defeat. The story as told by the Ngok Dinka is colorful and warrants quoting in detail. It was first introduced by Bulabek Malith, but only in the context of the rule against the ritual use of the Pajok sacred spears in wars with the black people. Bulabek said:

> The only time we pointed our spear at the black people was in the war at Ngol. There was an elder called Kwot Awet. His daughter was married to a Nuer. He told the Nuer, "If you have a double-tailed cow with the color *reng* [white with black stripes on the sides], you bring it and I will then give you my daughter." This Nuer went and found a reng cow with two tails. He brought this cow to Kwot and he said, "Can I now have the girl?" But Kwot said, "This reng cow and the girl, I will combine them." The Nuer saw this and attacked us. The fighting started from Ngol in a place called Akuoc. Then it came to Mijok Allor. The people of Acueng ran from a place called Nyongrial to a place called Mijok Allor, where the grave of our ancestor is. That is where an elder came and told the retreating people, "The sky has joined with the earth, you have nowhere else to go. If you run on, you will hit the sky." So the people faced the fight and held the front. At that point they chased the Nuer up to Dokura.
>
> The grandfather of Abiem told our grandfather, "We have found the Nuer. The cattle he captured at Ngol, he is now keeping at Miyan Koor. Tomorrow, if the war

starts, he will destroy all of us. Not even a chief will remain. Now they have killed Kwot Awet. Please point the spear at the Nuer." My grandfather said, "How can I point the sacred spear at the Nuer? The word has been passed down to us that we should not point the spear at black people." And Allor Ajing said, "If the Nuer kill us, our country will be without chiefs. Now they have killed Kwot, please point the sacred spear at them." Eventually, my grandfather called the country to bring a brown bull and a brown ram. They were brought.

He first sacrificed the brown ram and then killed the brown bull. He hit it with the spear—this sacred spear. He took the spear and pointed it at the brown bull as it went toward the Nuer. The Nuer were on a pool called Dokura. The brown bull ran up to Nuer area and fell among the Nuer. Suddenly the world turned into darkness so that the Nuer could not see the people. Those are the only black people at whom the sacred spear has ever been pointed.

The manner in which the ritual was carried out is of interest for it shows a Dinka religious practice whereby ritual or symbolic action is performed to achieve the immediately desired end while leaving no traces of guilt in the performer. By using the bull as the object, with the brown color symbolizing the Arab although they in effect intended it to signify the Nuer, the Dinka were able to inflict a ritual curse on the Nuer and eventually defeat them and yet remain at peace with the belief that they never in fact broke the prohibition of using the spears against the black man, for it was against the Arabs, symbolized by the bull, that the spears were ritually pointed. Thus, they both treated the Nuer as a foreign enemy for the purpose of achieving victory and yet continued to identify with them as their fellow black men.

The version given in the second Ngok interview was even

more sympathetic to the Nuer and perhaps for the same reason does not include the ritual use of the spear against them. Presumably in response to Marieu Ajak's statement that "it was the Arabs and the Nuer who destroyed the country," Chol Adija said, "In that war the Nuer were in the right." Loth Adija then proceeded to give a detailed explanation why.

It was the daughter of Kwot whom a Nuer married, the daughter of Kwot Awet. He married her with a hundred cows. And when she was married with a hundred cows, they said, "Now, give us the girl." Kwot Awet refused completely; he combined the cattle and his daughter. He said he would only give her away if they brought a cow with the color *reng*.

He said, "If you bring a reng with two tails, I will give you the girl." They went and searched for a reng with two tails until they found it. But again he combined the reng and the rest of the cattle with his daughter. The Nuer then said, "Kwot Awet, if we survive the night, we shall fight in the morning." They left without the cattle or the wife, and then attacked. They fought on the Ngol. And Chief Biong Allor was at the Kir River. Biong had told Kwot to give the girl to the Nuer and Kwot had refused. The sun suddenly disappeared into the clouds, and Biong said, "This sun which has disappeared into the clouds means that the Nuer have killed Kwot Awet."

Kwot had said, "I have a Mareng [the name of a sub-tribe and also the color pattern of a bull] which fights with both horns."

Acak [another sub-tribe] also bragged; they said they would teach the Nuer a lesson.

At this point Marieu Ajak took over:

Biong had said, "The land will spoil; give your daughter

away. If God has helped the Nuer to find a reng of two tails and they bartered it with eight cows, as it has truly happened, you give the girl away."

Kwot said, "No, I will not give her away."

Biong said, "But then the country will spoil!"

Kwot said, "My boys who carry shields are thirty; the Nuer will not destroy all of them."

Biong said, "So you will not listen to my words!?"

Kwot said, "No, I will not listen."

Biong therefore left him.

The Nuer were four; the Nuer who had come with the request returned. The cow with two tails had been sought throughout Nuerland. So all the Nuer without exception knew about the case; no one did not know. People asked, "What is the matter?"

They would say, "We married a girl for a hundred cows, but she is still withheld. The father says he wants a reng with two tails."

Then people asked, "And where can it be found?"

He went to that camp and to that camp and to that camp and to that camp. Then in Dok he found a reng with two tails. He brought her. And when the matter was discussed again, the Ngok refused. The Nuer were bewildered. They said, "Have the people returned empty-handed? Has the two-tailed reng been combined with the girl?"

They said, "Yes, she has been combined with the girl."

It was then said, "When the moon of Lal appears, all the Nuer, that's when we will attack. No one will tell anyone. Just as you see the moon appear, we shall follow the two-tailed reng. The Ngok have committed a wrong against us."

When the moon of Lal appeared, they moved. The attacking group grew and grew as they came.

Kwot had of course said, "I have thirty gentlemen

carrying shields and I am not mentioning the many younger ones. The Nuer will never destroy them all."

The Nuer came. The four gentlemen who had been courting the girl, each one said, "I shall not touch anybody else with my spear but Kwot Awet himself."

They carried their spears and drove a herd of oxen.

The Acak sub-tribe had eight divisions. They fought, and however much they fought, it was nothing to the Nuer. The Ngok were eventually forced to retreat. Kwot was then told, "The war is lost." The Nuer young men who knew Kwot's home ran through the fighting crowds heading for Kwot's home. They ran and ran and ran. The Nuer continued to kill the Ngok. Then the young men found Kwot. He was walking ahead of his daughter, who was carrying a gourd of milk with which her father occasionally wet his throat.

When they came, they first threw spears at the girl, their bride. She fell to the ground. Then they forced her father to the ground. They cut their throats, both of them. Then the world suddenly dimmed as the clouds covered the sky.

Biong then remarked, "Now that the sun is covered with clouds, they have killed Kwot; now that the sun has darkened, Kwot is dead."

The Nuer continued to destroy the country. That was how destruction came.

The manner in which all those present contributed to the story from this point on is worth noting for it shows once more both the wide sharing of oral history even to the details, and the creativity and possible distortion in the retelling process which the Dinka themselves recognize.

L. A. You are leaving out a small part; you should tell the rest.

C. A. He has cut the story.

L. A. The fighting was later resumed. The Ngok beat the war drums. And they met again with the Nuer. The Nuer again chased the Dinka. All those places like Maker and Dokura, they attacked and captured the herds. The Ngok reached Matuom near Merem, and then camped. When an elder called Ayom . . .

M. A. Ayom Biemngol; Ayom the brave.

L. A. Ayom Biemngol saw it; he thought and said, "This thing . . ."

M. A. "Our people are frightened."

L. A. "Our people are frightened. Our people are frightened. Only a few people are left."

C. A. He said, "Biong Wakbeek, I am going for a walk that way."

L. A. Yes, he bade the chief farewell and said he was going for a walk; "I shall return."

C. A. He said, "What I shall say, do not disagree with me."

M. A. "Our people are afraid."

L. A. Yes, he said, "Chief, do not disagree with me; our people are afraid. If only they get courageous enough, they can destroy the Nuer. And what will make them destroy the Nuer, I believe God has shown me. But chief, if you disagree with me then it will not work."

And he went for his walk. Then he returned in the evening. The cattle had been tethered. The Nuer were expected to attack the following morning.

M. A. He made his a word of God. . . .

L. A. Thus he returned to the camp at night.

At this point I had to intervene and plead for order, "May I say this. When two or more people speak at once, I later have difficulty in understanding from the tape what any one of them said." They appreciated my difficulty and permitted Loth to continue.

He came into the cattle-camp. He went onto a high plat-
form. Then he chanted his war song. As he chanted, the
whole camp became silent. Then he was asked, "Ayom,
what is the matter?"

He said, "Our people, look that way. Don't you see
that God [in the sky] has bent his head to the ground [at
the horizon]?"

People said, "Yes."

He said, "The earth and God have joined. They have
joined into a strong front. The world has come to a dead
end. We have reached the edge of the earth and there is
nowhere else to retreat. Come and see my axe. I tried to
cut through, but it was so hard it has bent the edge of the
axe. When I tried to cut through it with the axe, it
bled with blood. So let the cowards bury themselves
now. As for the brave, those who want to die with
their eyes fixed on the enemy, let no man dodge the
spears of the Nuer retreating from the Nuer; let them
dodge the spears advancing toward the Nuer and take
revenge for their own death. There is nowhere else to go;
the Nuer will only pierce our back to death where the
world has ended."

With those words and as the morning dawned and the
Nuer came, each man said to his wife, "The Nuer will
capture you where I cannot see or know." Each man said
to his children, "The Nuer will capture you where I
cannot see or know." Then the battle began, and the
Ngok advanced. You would dodge a Nuer spear and
pierce a Nuer with your spear. That is how the Ngok
destroyed the Nuer. They destroyed the Nuer and chased
them.

They advanced killing the Nuer and capturing their
cattle until they reached the place called Peny Nuer
[Nuer woodland]. They completely devastated the Nuer.
They captured Nuer cattle and recaptured the girls and

the children whom the Nuer had captured in earlier fights. That is how the saying started that Acueng tribe had said, "The world has come to an end."

Biong Allor asked, "Ayom, how did you think of this plan? By this thing you have truly helped me with the country. The Nuer would have completely destroyed my people."

To my question as to whether the wars between all the Dinka tribes and the Nuer were provoked by the case of Kwot Awet's daughter, Loth said:

Yes, it was the question of the girl which caused the fight . . . with all. . . . When they were defeated by the Ngok and their cattle were captured, they went and attacked the Twic. They destroyed the Twic and the Twic ran, coming into Ngokland. So the Nuer went and attacked the Jur Wir Dinka. Those Dinka would retreat into the river and escape from the Nuer. Then they proceeded to Apuk. That is how they fought. They also went to Paan Aruw.

While the Dinka are aware of their past hostilities with the Nuer, their main preoccupation is with the wars of slavery and conquest waged against them by waves of invaders whom they hardly distinguished, except by the use of such varied terms as the Arabs, the Turks, the Egyptians, the Ansars, or the Dongolawis. This phase of Sudanese history is a most sensitive one, the mention of which a great number of Sudanese, especially Northerners, consider treacherous to national unity. To the Southerners, however, it is a reality of recent history which may be forgiven but not forgotten.

Knowledge for knowledge's sake is a value which is often as intriguing as it is useful, and such usefulness is so inherent that it does not have to be visible or immediate. I believe that a distinction should be drawn between a discussion of past hostilities which aims at fanning further hostilities, and a realistic understanding of the way in which the past has conditioned the present so that we may anticipate and counteract predictable negatives in our plans for the future. Although the South-North problem has now been solved, such a strategy, if mutually appreciated, promises even better results for the future. The solution is in effect not an end but only the beginning of a constructive march toward the ultimate end of peace-consolidation and nation-building.

Condominium

Despite the official designation of the Condominium as Anglo-Egyptian, the partnership essentially meant British rule with Egypt as a rubber-stamp half. One of the remarkable achievements of British rule in the Sudan is the way it won the confidence of the Southern tribes to the point of blinding them to the negatives of colonialism. The developmental deprivations it imposed on the South in comparison to the North, and the eventual unconditional handing over of the Southern minority to the dominance of the North consequently provoked the South into a devastating civil war that became reminiscent of the pre-Condominium hostilities. Ironically, the British won the confidence of the Southern tribes by terminating "Arab-Negro" hostilities, yet their rule in the Sudan came to an end under conditions which appeared to the Dinka quite comparable to the "spoiled world" of the pre-colonial era.

Because of the disruptive conditions the British found in the Sudan, their main objective was to establish and maintain peace and security through law and order. However, so subjected to varied forms of unscrupulous foreign invasions were the Southern tribes that they would not trust the British despite their professed mission to rid the tribes of those earlier ills. After all, to the Southerners the Mahdists had come initially veiled as saviors, only to be unveiled as slavers, deceitful and destructive. Thus apprehensive and mistrustful, the Southerners first resisted British rule and the government was faced with uprisings in many tribes. It was not until the late twenties that some tribes began to see the British as advocates of peace and security and therefore more as benefactors than malefactors. And, indeed, whatever can be said against British rule in the Sudan, it brought the longest period of peace and security, at least from invasion and the use of crude force, that has been experienced in the South throughout recorded history. The unfaltering faith and confidence they won for that is more than abundantly supported by the accounts in the interviews.

A number of these accounts present British intervention in the Sudan as motivated by the desire to save the black man from Arab slavers. In view of the pre-Condominium pressures by European missionaries on the British government and the role the British government played in suppressing slavery throughout the Turko-Egyptian rule, there is reason to believe that this view is not an afterthought.

According to Chief Makuei Bilkuei:

> The Mahdi took the people and sold them to the Egyptians. The Egyptians took the people and sold them to the white people. That is when the English came and said, "This black man who can talk, what brings him to me here?" That's when the English got up and said, "We have to go and see what brings the black man here." They traveled, crossing the territory, and traveled and traveled until they found Juba and Uganda.

According to Chief Thon Wai, "As we heard it from our fathers, and then we saw it with our own eyes, it was the thing that sold our people which brought the English."

Marieu Ajak elaborates the process by which the attention of the British was drawn to the plight of the black man and some of the alleged deceitful tactics the Arabs used by arguing that the black man sold himself into slavery.

> The Arab would come here [to the North] and sell the people away. And he would be asked, "Where does this black man come from?" He would answer, "There is a black race there which sells themselves. Each man comes and says, 'Father, I want you to put me up for auction.' Even young girls, and women who had newly given birth, and young men!"

Chief Makuei presents the English as "brought" by the chiefs to rescue their people and elaborates on the consequences of their intervention.

> It is our fathers—people like Bilkuei, people like Kwol Arob—who brought the English. So it is because of the English that some people were saved. They ended the war. And then we paid taxes. The English then said to us, "Build your homes." So we started building our homes and settling down.
>
> So, what brought the English was the indignity the Ansar were inflicting upon us. If there had been no problem with the Ansar, the English would not have come. If no one had been taken away to be sold, the English would not have come.

Chief Thon Wai also makes the same point of the British coming in defense of the South, ending the wars of slavery, and bringing peace.

> That was what we heard and saw. The English came because they heard of what the Egyptians and the Ansar had done to us. So they came to step between us and those people who had troubled us. The Englishman came to help. It is just that he did not educate us. He educated the people of the North but did not educate us.

As for removing the war, he did help a lot, saying, "These people still do not know anything and should not be left to be victims of those who know something." He removed the war between us so that we would stay as persons and know each other as people.

Chief Stephen Thongkol went beyond the British establishment of peace to speak of the development the British introduced to the traditional society.

And when the British came, they stopped us from fighting and told us, "You South and you North, you will unite to be one person; you will have one government." Then the English introduced us to education. The South accepted writing and began to learn bit by bit. At first they learned in Dinka, and after they learned Dinka some went ahead and started learning English. That is how we entered the government. When the white man introduced us to education, our people began to collect boys to be sent to school. They were collected as though they were taxes.

Thus, while the view is generally held that the British governed the Sudan under a system of divide and rule, and indeed they kept the South and the North separate during most of their rule, the accounts of the Dinka emphasize the opposite, namely that it was the British rule which brought the Northerners and the Southerners together and united them. This point is especially stressed by Ngok chiefs and elders. The words of Chief Biong Mijak are illustrative. "We now live together with the Arabs because of the work of the English. And even when our money went to the North in payment of taxes, it was said to be because we were in one country in which the English had established peace and abolished quarrels."

This paradox, of Northerners feeling that it was the British who divided the country and Southerners taking the opposite argument that it was the British who united it, can be explained through the British policy of indirect rule. Considering the logistics involved in governing after the disruption of the pre-Condominium era, the British found it both economically and politically prudent to rule through tribal chiefs and traditional institutions. Where chiefs had disappeared they were sought and reinstated or simply replaced with other persons who had emerged from the ruins as the leaders of their people through their own charisma, generosity, or influence. The chiefs I interviewed are nearly all descendants of chiefs who ascended through one or another of these alternative criteria, and are by definition allies of the British colonial system. This is worth considering in evaluating their positive view of the British. But the representative quality of the chiefs' view of the British cannot be explained merely by reference to the subjectivity of the chiefs as an interest group. Much of the explanation of the group attitude lies in the fact that ruling through the chiefs was only an aspect of a much wider policy of leaving the tribes to themselves as much as possible, not assuming any significant responsibility for their development, except for minor educational concessions to the missionaries, and not opening doors too wide for cross-racial, or urban-rural interaction which might have the effect of disrupting the tranquility and the convenience of insulated traditional orders. For the Dinka, whose ethnocentric view of themselves is second to none and whose contact with the outside world had brought little but devastation and dehumanization, this "splendid isolation" was far from deprivation; it was the ideal for which they were appreciative and grateful.

The positive view of the Dinka about the British goes beyond their policies and administrative virtues and extends to the evaluation of the British as a people and as individuals in idealized terms, focusing on their uprightness, honesty, and dignity. According to Chief Giirdit:

> The Dinka saw the English as a good man. He is not the man who would give you anything nor do anything to help you go ahead, but he is a good man. He would not cheat you of your thing. The English may eat your thing, but he would do so hiding it cleverly and not indiscreetly. A man who takes somebody else's thing indiscreetly, showing it to the people, is bad. He is not a noble man. But a man who takes advantage of somebody else in a discreet way is not bad. The English, if he sees your thing fallen among his things, he will pick it out and give it to you. But if it were these neighbors of ours, instead of giving it back, they would cover it with many other things in order to cheat you.

Speaking of Americans and identifying them with the British, Chief Ayeny Aleu said: "It is their race that will one day be our good friends. As for this other race here, which says one word up there and other words go on underneath here, so that you laugh with a person but with other things hidden inside you, that is not the race for us." In a later context, Chief Ayeny Aleu, still identifying the Americans with the English, went further to reveal the deep sense of identification and commitment the traditionalists feel toward the British, even to the point of betraying the dignity of independence and concealing the bondage of colonialism, which was too disguised from them to notice or too outweighed by the evils of the pre- and post-colonial disruptions to be viewed as constraining.

> Their main mistake is that they did not educate us; if only they had educated us above the Arabs! They were deceived by the Arabs who murmured into their ears saying, "If you educate these people, they will take the country from both of us." And they listened to the

words of the Arabs and agreed to what they said. If they had educated us before the Arabs, they would still be here today. But they went ahead and educated thieves. That is why the Arabs came and sent them away. Now, they come back only as guests. This is the race which in the past, when we saw them, they had charisma. And we, these people who are so black, so different from them, we are similar with them.

In his admiration of the British, Chief Arol Kacwol, like Chief Ayeny, goes as far as lamenting the departure of the British from the Sudan: "When they, the white people, left this country, we were mourning their departure. We were saying that the people who were being left with us were not really our relatives and that the white man was someone we had been very happy with. We saw them as our relatives."

Of course, as is apparent in the words of Chiefs Thon Wai and Ayeny Aleu about the British not having given the South education, or in the rather tolerant words of Chief Giirdit about the English not being generous but indeed discreetly "eating" other people's things, the Dinka praise for the British is not without minor reservations. However, of all the people interviewed, only Chief Yusuf Deng, whose Islamic cultural outlook gives him something of a Northern-type sophistication, is ambivalently critical of British rule in the Sudan. While most Dinkas blame the British only for not having developed or educated the South, Chief Yusuf, though generally the most critical of the British, exonerates them on the issue of education, placing the blame on the Southerners themselves.

When the English came, they did not educate us. But our ignorance did not come from the English. It was already there and it was part of our people's mentality. We hear, for instance, that the English wanted to take children to schools and our fathers refused. They would call on the

chiefs to send their children to school and each one
would say, "I have no other child to take care of the
cattle and the sheep and goats." So I think the mistake
was that of our fathers.

As is evident from the foregoing accounts, the view of Dinka chiefs about the British is almost uniformly and unsophis-
ticatedly positive. The reason is obvious. The Dinka are a part
of a Negroid complex of peoples and cultures which, while
partaking from, and presumably contributing to, the melting-
pot of cultures along the Nile Valley, have also suffered waves
of invasion and brutalization, which seem to have been unin-
terrupted for centuries until the intervention of the British
in the very late nineteenth century—in effect, decades into
the twentieth century. To the Dinka, therefore, the British
are the source of the peace, security, and dignity that known
history has given them. This has blinded the Dinka to the
British shortcomings whose consequences paradoxically
plunged the country, and especially the South, into a civil
war almost as grave in magnitude as the upheaval from which
the British had extricated them in the first place.

Independence

As will already have become apparent in the foregoing sections, the independence movement in the Sudan was started
and carried out almost entirely by the Northern Sudanese,
with the support of Egypt which hoped for unity between
the Sudan and Egypt after independence. Although the
Southern voice, and finally vote, were crucial to the ultimate
attainment of full independence under a system of unconditional unity, the nationalist movement came and progressed
considerably at a time when the South had not yet awakened
politically.

The Juba Conference in 1946, which marked the turning
point in British policy toward the South, was perhaps the

first visible step toward Southern involvement. The British had decided to follow a unitary policy toward the South and develop the area as rapidly as they could to enable Southerners to have a fair share in an independent Sudan, then closely in sight as the forces of independence were marching relentlessly toward their ultimate goal. It was at the protest of the British administrators in the South to the new policy, and on their suggestion that the Southerners be consulted, that the Juba Conference was convened, to gauge Southern opinion on the issue of whether the South should participate with the North in a legislative assembly, which was to be formed, or should have their own regional legislature. The issue of unity was by and large assumed and the inclusive legislative assembly was to be a step toward that unity.

The conference included British colonial representatives, Northern Sudanese, Southern chiefs, and civil servants. To begin with, the consensus of Southern opinion was that although the Sudan was one country, the South was still far behind the North in political development, and therefore should have a separate advisory council until they were sufficiently developed to have their own legislative assembly on an equal footing with the North. Under intensive activity from Northern representatives, however, the educated Southern representatives altered their position on the second day of the conference and favored full participation in the all-Sudan legislative assembly. The tribal chiefs remained firm on their earlier views.

In deciding to participate with the Northerners in the legislative assembly, the educated Southerners were paradoxically relying on the colonial government to safeguard their interests and protect them from the North, should the latter prove to be dominating the South. Thus, when one British official asked a leading Southern participant at the conference "what his safeguard would be if, in spite of the

Southern objections in the Legislative Assembly, a law was passed which was against the interest of the Southerners," he replied that "the government would protect him."[2]

Subsequent events happened in very rapid succession. The Legislative Assembly for the whole Sudan opened on December 15, 1948, with Southern representatives, and on February 12, 1953, the Anglo-Egyptian Agreement was concluded, to liquidate Condominium rule and introduce self-rule as a step toward self-determination. From then on, Southern political consciousness was awakened. Southerners began to call first for a form of regional autonomy and later for federation. But events proceeded relentlessly toward independence and, with that procession, Southern fear of domination by the North intensified. With the announcement of the results of the Sudanization of posts previously held by the colonial powers, and of which the Southerners received a negligible number, Southern opposition and fear were fanned into the violent revolt of August 1955 which ignited the civil war that was to last for seventeen years.

However, despite their grievances and the then still limited revolt in the form of mutiny, the South ultimately supported the independence of the country on the Northern promise that the Southern call for a federal system would be given "full consideration." The motion for the declaration of independence was seconded by a Southerner and was adopted unanimously. The Sudan formally became independent on January 1, 1956.

Subsequent attempts to solve the Southern problem came to no avail. Efforts at agreeing on a permanent constitution were fruitless. Governments came and went, sometimes intensifying, sometimes relaxing their grip on the South, then caught up in a spreading fire of civil war. Southern strength improved with outside help and although the military wing of

2. Sudan Government, *Southern Sudan Disturbances* (1956) quoted in Deng, *Dynamics of Identification*, p. 36.

the movement, the Anya-Nya, could not defeat the government security forces, neither could it be defeated. The result of the stalemate was terrorism for the civilian population in the South, the breakdown of public order, and the stagnation, indeed retardation, of economic development.

But the situation was not static. A process of political restructuring was under way. The dynamics of intergenerational conflicts, and the more modern disposition of both Northern and Southern youth as compared to their respective traditional leaders, brought about trends toward self-examination and the search for broader bases for national identification. This was also aided by other conditions such as the tide of nationalism in Africa; the increased pride in African heritage; the discovery of similarities, racial and cultural, between Northern Sudanese and many other Africans who called themselves "African" if not "Negro"; the realization of significant differences in racial and cultural characteristics between the Northern Sudanese and other Arabs; and not least, the adverse effects of the long civil war. In all this the young educated Sudanese led his elders. It was he who, as a student or official, traveled abroad under circumstances that fostered close relations with the outside world and who observed the complexities of racial identification, the backwardness of official policies in this regard, and the need for accelerating social and economic development. It was the young people who were called "black" or "Negro" when they went to Arab countries or to certain racially mixed countries and who experienced the shock of not being considered Arab. In some Arab countries, Northerners were even called "abid" (slave). Their shock led to self-discovery and a more meaningful realization of the complexities of Sudanese identity. These developments are remarkably fitted into the historical context in a poem addressed to a fictitious Southerner, Malual, by Salah Ahmad Ibrahim, former Ambassador of the Sudan to Algeria.

I quote from this poem in some detail because it captures
the essence of South-North history, reveals the complexities of Sudanese identity, and articulates the challenges
facing the Sudanese in the process of nation-building. After
verses in which he vows to tell the truth, he continues with
the history:

> Malual, before you deny me
> Listen to my story of the South and the North
> The story of enmity and brotherhood from ancient
>   times
> The Arab, the carrier of the whip, the driver of
>   the camels
> Descended on the valleys of the Sudan like the
>   summer rains
> With the Book and the ways of the Prophet. . . .
> Carrying in his leather bag his ambitions and his
>   plates
> And two dates and his ancestral tree. . . .
> A reality blossomed in the womb of every slave woman
>   of a free man
> The progeny of your Arab ancestors
> Among them were the Fur and the Funj
> And all those who are charcoal black
> A reality as large as the elephant and like the crocodile
> And like the high mountains of Kassala. . . .
> He lies who says in the Sudan
> That I am pure
> That my ancestry is not mixed
> That my ancestry is not tinted
> He is truly a liar. . . .[3]

The struggle over power between the older elements of con-

---

3. From a collection entitled *Ghadhbat Al-Hababai* (1965). From an informal
translation quoted in F. M. Deng, *Dynamics of Identification* (Khartoum, Khartoum University Press, 1973), pp. 69–70.

servatism and the younger forces of change, and the discovery of the racial and cultural complexities of the Sudan, together with the determination of the South to fight for its recognition, encouraged opposition among the youth as well as certain other elements in the North. These groups had previously been overshadowed under the embracing umbrella of Arab-North and left powerless, undeveloped, content with simply the label. A complex process of alignment and realignment between Northern youth, certain disenchanted ethnic groups in the North, and the Southern Sudanese began to threaten the system. It was the leadership of university students and young faculty members with the support of young military officers that led to the popular October 1964 uprising which forced the Abboud military regime to resign. The leaders of the coup, however, being idealistic, permitted public elections, which soon brought back into power the conservative leaders of party politics.

Such was the situation until the May 1969 Revolution led by Jaafar Nimeri. Shortly after seizing power, the revolutionary leaders declared autonomy for the South, but its implementation was initially impeded by the ideological prerequisites then regarded as necessary for regional autonomy in the South. Despite the declaration of autonomy, therefore, hostilities continued and even intensified. A dramatic move to break with the past was made following the abortive communist coup of January 1971. With Nimeri's victorious return to power after three days of uncertainty, events moved very fast toward the settlement of the Southern problem. Intensive diplomatic activity between the parties to the conflict and intermediaries ended in the Addis Ababa discussions between the Southern Liberation Movement and the Sudan Government, hosted by Emperor Haile Selassie, who himself played a pivotal role in making the talks succeed. The result was the Addis Ababa Accord which gives the South regional autonomy within a united Sudan,

164 CONTACT WITH OUTSIDERS

and which has been implemented with surprising smoothness. With the help of the international community, the Sudan has welcomed back one million Southerners who were in exile or displaced in the forests of the South and has been able to give them relief and to resettle and rehabilitate them. This achievement, after seventeen years of bitter and devastating conflict, is almost unprecedented and although it was first viewed with serious doubts for its success, it is now accepted as a reality, despite difficulties and continued apprehensions.

This skeleton review of the history of South-North relations, from the independence movement to the end of the civil war, is given flesh by the accounts in the interviews. The near-consensus view of those interviewed, and one which further illustrates their idealization of the British, is that the British should not have gone. Their premature departure is seen as the result of maneuvers and misleading tactics by the Egyptians and the Northerners against the Southerners, who were too immature in the political arena and therefore fell easy prey. Chief Makuei Bilkuei, after tracing the more distant history of Mahdism in Dinkaland continued:

> What I heard is that Egypt said to the people in Khartoum, "This white man must go. You people are educated enough to take over." He said it to Azhari and Abdalla Khalil. Mohammed Naguib called them and said, "From Mading Aweil to Juba to Torit, let us all unite and let us send the English away. We will control our country to be called the Sudan." It was Mohammed Naguib and Ismail El Azhari, and Abdalla Khalil who started to court us. They courted us and said, "Let us unite our words; let us unite our mouths to be one people." That is how we united. But soon afterwards we started to fight like bulls.

Asked what the chiefs thought of the Southern decision to unite with the North and obtain independence for the Sudan,

Makuei restated a position similar to that of the chiefs at the Juba Conference and placed the blame for what happened on the educated Southerners.

> When it was first started, I was there. People from America came, two of them. They came and said, "You people, you Beir and you Nuer and you Dinka, come! Should the English go or do you disagree that the English go?" We said, "The English should not go. If the English go now, we are still going to come back and we will start fighting again. And we will be insulted. We will be called 'slaves,' 'dogs,' 'fools.' We will not be allowed to sit on seats or on beds."
>
> So, it is you the educated who destroyed our country. It was you the educated who brought us into this situation. I, Makuei, I said, "let us be educated first; let the English not go yet. All the blacks from Rek to Rumbek to Torit, let us be educated first and let the English leave when we are educated. What has now come through Egypt, you people will see red blood." That was what I said, and it has now come true.

Many chiefs present the cause of the conflict as the failure by the North to recognize basic economic, political, and cultural inequities between the South and the North. Chief Thon Wai expressed this view in the following words:

> If a man gives a goat—let us say I, Thon, give one goat to one of my sons and I give ten cows to another son. The son to whom I give a goat will not be satisfied. Each day will come and a fight will erupt. And in the end the suffering will reach me, the man who first made the decision. Why should I give one son a goat and give ten cows to the other son? That is my fault and that fault will one day come back to me. The day the judgment is made, people will say, "Thon, it is you who put the children in conflict. Why did you give a goat to one child

and the other child you gave ten cows? Why did you think of it? It was you who put them in conflict." The blame would come back to me. They are both my children. Why should I give one son cows and the other a goat? That is a mistake. And that is what brings conflict.

If the government, our brothers called the Northerners, had thought and said, "Take this, brother, it is big enough; and you brother, take this, it is big enough"; thus giving equal shares to all, we would have had nothing to quarrel about. Our conflict would have ended a long time ago.

According to Chief Thon, correcting this inequity was a matter of urgency which the North failed to realize: "What made us fall apart is such talk as, 'Wait, you will eat tomorrow.' But what if one should suddenly die? What if one suddenly died in the middle of the night? One would no longer get what one was supposed to wait for. What we want is that all of us should have a bit in our mouths. And if we should die in the middle of the night, then so be it. That was what we wanted." Instead, according to Chief Thon Wai, complaints are answered with "'This will be seen later. It will be seen tomorrow.' This, 'It will be seen tomorrow,' is what is destroying our country. The thing called 'It will be seen tomorrow' is the thing which is destroying the country." And in a later context, he continued his attack on the postponing disposition of *baadeen* "later" and "tomorrow."

What has always angered our hearts, we the chiefs of the tribes, is this thing called *baadeen, baadeen, baadeen; baadeen* makes the whole world go astray. With *baadeen*, a man may leave and never return. He will have gone angry. He will go back to his cattle-byre saying, "Why should I continue to run after that!" And it was not food he was running after; it was only a word, a word which would tell him that he was wrong if he were wrong; or

if he did not go wrong, a word which would tell him that
he had acted right. And this other thing called "tomorrow," "tomorrow" is what is destroying this country
and it is what is dividing our country.

Chief Yusuf Deng also said the following on the issue of
social justice and the urgency of its realization:

So, what we are saying is if our brother has cultivated
first and his crops have ripened and he is the first to hold
a thing in his hands, we say, "Let us share what you
have." . . . But if one says that he is to have a big share
while giving a small share to the other, that is what we
objected to and that is what led to the conflict. Those
who needed more said, "We are entitled to more; we will
not accept this. We have the right." And it is a man's
right which makes him speak up. Today, as we speak, if
I did not have a right, I would not be here saying all this.

The form the civil war took and the magnitude of Southern
suffering is another theme on which many accounts focus.
According to Chief Thon Wai:

Our brothers, in their anger with us, harassed all those
people who remained at home, including their chiefs.
Even if the people of the forest had only passed near a
camp, they would come and say, "They are here inside
the camp." They would proceed to destroy the camp.
Children would die and women would die. The chief
would only stand holding his head. If you tried force,
you fell a victim. Whatever you tried, you fell a victim.
Nothing made it better. You just sat mourning with
hands folded like a woman.

Chief Ayeny Aleu described the experience thus:

The terrible things that have happened in this area, if I
were to take you around and guide you around the

whole South, to see the bones of men lying in the forest, to see houses that were burned down, villages that were set on fire, to see this and that, you would leave without asking me; you would leave without saying, "Is this how we were living in our country?" You would leave without saying, "Is this how the South has turned out?" You would be dead silent; you would not ask me a single question.

Referring to the Juba mass murder of 1965, one of the worst tragedies of the civil war, and the assassination of the Southern nationalist, William Deng, Chief Yusuf Deng said:

Here in Juba, a lot of our educated men were destroyed. It was all a plan from our brothers. People cried, but it was as though they would return. That one man of ours who stood up and said, "Let us do something and share our land justly," the man called William, we know how he went. It was all part of a plan, the plan of our brothers. That, we hated. That a man should say "Let us share," and be destroyed, angered us. What killed a man with brave eyes, a man who knew something, we hated.

Chief Thon described the art by which those who remained at home survived.

When some of us refused to run, we said, "We cannot all go to the forest. To whom shall we leave our country?" So, we remained at home. Whenever the boys came in the middle of the night, they would find food, they would find cattle, they would find a goat, they would eat but then leave. If any one of us was caught, he would say, "This is a man from the forest, how do I know him? He is a man with a gun, and I have only a spear. How could I fight him? Guns destroy. Spears do not destroy." We would explain it that way. That is how we lived, avoiding one another, crossing our paths, each man coming and the other going.

Despite the agony they have gone through, the bitterness they feel against the North, and the apprehensions they hold about the future, Southerners deeply value the settlement of the Southern problem and glorify the leadership that made it possible. Their appreciation is particularly focused on the person of President Nimeri who is viewed not only as the man who made the settlement possible but also as the only one the South can rely upon for continued support and protection from the North. In the words of Chief Ayeny Aleu:

> He alone, Nimeri alone, is the man. If he should fall, if Nimeri falls, then we, the Southerners, are dead—we are completely dead. If another Arab were to seize the seat of power, then that's it; we are finished on this earth. If that happens, even I, all I will need is to be given a gun; and even if I cannot shoot it, I will take it and go into the forest with it. If Nimeri were to fall, we would break it off; we would definitely break it off; there would be no further relationship between us and the Northerners.

Chief Stephen Thongkol put it thus:

> The war has not ended; the problem has not ended. It is Nimeri who is containing it. If Nimeri were not here, people would die. If any small thing should happen to Nimeri, we are dead. If it is in the heart of God and he keeps Nimeri alive, we will be all right; but if Nimeri goes, we will die.

Yusuf Deng, after describing the suffering the South has experienced at the hands of the North, continued, "If a good man called Sayed Jaafar Mohammed El Nimeri has now come and said, 'This man has a right,' then we know that he is the only man who has seen our truth. That one man, we must praise."

According to Chief Thon Wai:

> Today, our people have accepted Nimeri. Why have they
> accepted him? It is because he has realized that the
> people of the South should be given the opportunity
> they are asking for. Only if they are given the oppor-
> tunity will the war end. If it is not given to them, the war
> will never end. He hit at the truth. He is the son of a
> man whose heart is alive. And he is the son of a man
> with open eyes. When his father was born and when his
> mother was born and when he himself was born, they
> were born with alert hearts.

> He looked into it and said, "Brothers in the North, this
> is not going to end. Let us give our brothers in the South
> a small piece and we remain with a small piece. Let us
> eat here and let them eat there. A man who will prefer
> to eat in the North will eat in the North. A man who will
> prefer to eat in the South will come and put his hand in
> the dish of the South. We will eat together and share."

To the Dinka, the wisdom to know what is bad is as good
as being morally inclined. And ironically, although the Dinka
ordinarily associate manhood with violence, physical courage,
and strength, the belief in the superiority of persuasive
authority to coercive power, when it comes to leadership,
makes them speak of Nimeri as "a man" for ending the civil
war. According to Chief Giirdit, "This Nimeri is a man; he
is a man for having brought reconciliation."

Chief Arol Kacwol goes further to speak of God having picked up "the man" called Nimeri and given him the
"strength" to hate death.

> Then God saw it all and he asked for the man called
> Nimeri. He went and looked for the man called Nimeri,
> a man like you people. He picked him up and gave him
> the strength with which to reconcile people. He gave him
> the strength to hate death. What was so difficult be-
> tween the North and the South, he managed.

As is apparent in the foregoing words of Chief Thon Wai, some people believe Nimeri's action to have been a shrewd pragmatic move based on the realization that the war was far too costly, with no foreseeable end or advantage, Chief Thon Wai emphasized what he saw as the pragmatism of Nimeri's action.

> When Jaafar Nimeri did what he did, he was doing nothing extraordinary. He only saw the chronic disease which was affecting everybody, including the North. He saw a chronic problem which kept them lean, year after year, like the rains which do not stop falling year after year. He saw that the Southerners might be killed today, but tomorrow others would rise and the rain of war would continue to fall. More would be killed and yet others would rise and the rain would fall. We might all finish and our children too might finish but the rain would continue to fall with the children of our children. And no one would enjoy power over the other.
>
> As long as we, the Southerners, were on fire, the whole Sudan would suffer from the heat of the burning fire. We would all be victims. A man on fire cannot enjoy the pleasure of power. But a man in a cool place feels the pleasure of power, a power in which no one pierces you and pierces you; pierces your back and pierces your feet. Then you can sleep.

For some people, the virtue of Nimeri's action is above power politics—indeed, it is above ordinary human capability. For these people, Nimeri must have supernatural qualities to do what he did. Chief Ayeny Aleu made this point in procreational terms to conclude that Nimeri must have been conceived by God directly and not merely by a man and a woman, his parents.

> This one man called Nimeri was created by God; I must say he was created by God. He was not just born of a woman. His grandfather, Nimeri, has done nothing in

this country. And his own father, Mohammed, has done nothing in the Sudan. When Jaafar came on his own, he saw the country and did that which stopped blood from flowing. A man like that is not a man borne by a woman. If he were born as an integral part of the North, if he were a Northerner, he could never have seen things the way he saw them. We see him as a man who was born directly of God; God created him and put him in the midst of all of us to help us straighten our backs and strengthen ourselves. That man called Nimeri, I do not know where God picked him from and placed him there on the top! It is now because of Nimeri that other countries look to us with respect. Before him, this was a country of misery.

In view of the animosity, the brutality, the bitterness, and the suspicion Southerners have experienced in their relations with the North, not only in the recent past, but for the major part of their remembered history, the peaceful manner in which the settlement of the Southern problem was achieved and the national accommodation, cooperation, and solidarity that have marked at least the relations of their respective leaderships since, were predictable by a few only in the very long run and by most people not at all. For the same reason, Southerners have come to appreciate and glorify Nimeri as uniquely understanding and generous to the South, and for the Southern masses, he is the divine gift, a hero, the like of whom has never appeared in the history of their country and is hardly ever to be expected again. This is a commitment which is as unanimous and powerful in the South as it is feared and resented in certain circles, especially in the North, as it makes hopes for the future of national unity so dependent on the survival of the one man.

4. Building the Nation

Under the heading of nation-building, I propose to consider three specific topics: consolidation of peace and unity, promotion of social and economic development, and prospects for national integration.

Unity

The manner in which the seventeen-year-old civil war was peacefully ended indicates what has been a remarkable shift in political dynamics. The Southern Movement was an opposition to unity in the old system, with some Southerners calling for various forms of regionalism or federation and others for total separation, all of which the North considered degrees of the same thing—separatism. To the Southerners, on the other hand, the very word "unity" was synonymous with domination by the North. Today, leaders on both sides acclaim unity not only as a goal attained in the achievement of peace, but as a value to be continuously pursued, consolidated, and maintained. Implicit in this call is a deep-rooted feeling of uncertainty or doubt about the reality or durability of unity and therefore of peace, for without unity there is no peace and without peace there can be no unity. This delicate equation is the foremost concern not only of the leaders on both sides but also of the Southern populace.

The situation in reality today provides for both unity and separatism and it is precisely because it combines these seemingly opposed phenomena that it has such an appeal to the South and to at least the crucial elements of Northern leadership. According to the system, Southerners can participate on two levels, the regional and the national. The law governing this system is, as are all fundamental laws, phrased broadly enough to allow a margin of discretion. Ultimately, it largely depends on the national leadership, and particularly the President, whether regional autonomy is given wide or restricted operation. With the unquestioned support of the national leadership for the Southern cause, the present application of autonomy tends to be extensive, if only on matters not vital or sensitive to the character of the nation. Nonetheless, and by the same token, this implies a willing regional dependency on the center. Partly because of the centrifugal forces exerted by the President's authority and partly because of the importance of the center for crucial matters— such as handling international relations, on which depends much of the financial and technological input for development—regional participation is largely channeled through the controlling, though seemingly remote, hands of the center. For various reasons, this process is also characterized by Southern interpersonal or intergroup competition and sometimes by intrigues aimed at securing greater influence in the region and/or the center.

A complex situation is thus created where unity is unanimously avowed and regionalism is conceived as conferring extensive powers; but paradoxically the regionalism is dependent on central support and therefore centrally controlled. This is likely to encourage, if subtly, central absorption of the autonomous South. As the Sudanese, especially Southerners, may be largely unaware of this subtle process, they are not adequately equipped or prepared to consciously promote Southern influence on this assimilating or integrating process. The result is that Southern influence on the national character is likely to be a diffuse outcome of the process rather than the product of a planned dynamic mutual assimilation.

The foregoing analysis shows that the solution of the Southern problem may in effect be a step, and for that matter a giant step, in the direction of a long-range solution. That ultimate solution would seem to imply integration if national unity is a prerequisite, and if diversity and its attendant discrepancy are acknowledged as the sources of disunity and conflict. We shall later discuss the prospects for such integration, but at this juncture it is opportune to review the basic trends of the chiefs' views on the prospects of consolidating peace and unity.

On the whole, the chiefs regard the solution as both ideal and obvious in the sense that it was the only way the problem could have been amicably resolved. For the same reason, they regard autonomy as a compromise solution but, at the same time, adequate. According to Chief Albino Akot, the adequacy of the solution and its acceptability to the South have to be balanced against the possible political alternative move by the North. The following was in answer to a question about how he viewed the future of the settlement.

> Well, by God, this is a difficult question. The political situation of the Sudan today is a bit complicated. With the new system which has just been started, we watch and ask ourselves, "Will it work well so that people come, inspect, and know that what was sought has been found, or will this turn out to be different? How are we going to stay together knowing what we have done and are doing?"
>
> Our side, we Southerners, we have no fear because we are people who are following one way. Whatever we say, we do. What we have accepted, we will follow. From the point of view of the Southern Sudan I do not think there will be any problem.
>
> What will bring trouble is the Northern Sudan. That is where the problem will start. And if that problem should affect the Southern Sudan, the position of the South will be different from what it is now; it will be completely different. Why will it be different? Because, if you look

into the North, you will see that they want alternatives to the system which is now existing there. They want to change it into what they really want in their own hearts and not what we have agreed upon together. They will find the situation different when they do that; our position will differ from their position.

We do not know what strength we will have. If we do have strength, nothing will make us join their way. Their way will be their way and we will have our own way. We will have our own chance to stand by ourselves. We do not have the intention to start any trouble. We do not want it to be said that it is we who want to break away. What we wanted we have now found. What little has been given to us, we have accepted. We are quiet with it.

Now we have finished the bad side, nobody wants to think of the past; nobody wants to bring it back. There are a few elements in the South who may still think that this is too small. Those we can overcome. What cannot be easily overcome is that which will come from the North.

Chief Lino Aguer spoke of the situation as primarily one of an ended feud which of necessity leaves its scars of bitterness that cannot easily disappear and the full amicability of which can only be acknowledged after the fact rather than predicted.

With respect to hatreds, no man can really say. If it is not the word of God, who can say what will be? People with hatred befriend one another but they do not sleep well. If one sleeps near the other, he may sleep but he opens his eyes quickly and looks around because he is a man with whom there is a feud. Whatever you do together, you have a feud between yourselves. If they stay a long time and cool down and stay as friends, you may then talk about it as a story. People will then refer to it saying, "We thought it would happen again, but it has not happened." I cannot really tell now whether it will go well or spoil; I cannot tell you.

Chief Thon Wai, following the same line of thought, also considers it difficult to predict unity, and prefers a wait-and-see attitude.

So, we and our brothers, the time when we will unite and live together is known to God alone. We will not say it ourselves. Why won't we say it? It is because we have had some experience. An old man, in fact an uncle of mine, said, "The future is unknown." Yes, the future is unknown. Nobody knows what life is ahead. Nobody knows what will come in the morning.

But even in this wait-and-see period. he views the South and North as so different that they must maintain a certain distance to remain at peace:

Our life with the North is like that of a cold egg and a hot egg. The sun is hot and the moon is cold. They keep their distance from one another. They do not meet. They act as though they are about to meet but they miss one another. Then they go on as though wanting to meet, but they miss again and again.

Chief Stephen Thongkol, after presenting the solution as the result of political pragmatism on the side of the North, proceeded to list grievances that make it difficult for him to consider the problem solved or unity achieved.

The war is going on. We cannot say we are relatives. The war is still on. There is no relationship. How does your relationship with them come about? Here we are, called Southerners! Many bad things are already evident. For instance, our children are being prevented from learning English in school. Respect toward people is missing. Our chiefs don't have a salary that is respectable. We are still being insulted. Some people still call us slaves; some of us are still actually slaves. We cannot marry their daughters. They take our girls and turn them into prostitutes, and when they have made them prostitutes they send them back. They are still controlling our economy: they are the people who own the shops, and all the money is still in their hands. The only thing which has improved is the area of security. This is slightly improved. But everything else is still in their hands. They still have the voice and they still have the whip.

Southerners are only children. If they are told that this has gone well, they celebrate and sing and say, "Oh, it's wonderful, it's wonderful," and they don't know what is going on.

Thus, Southerners do not rule out problems and indeed call upon their fellow Southerners to exert great caution toward and keen observation of the situation. Chief Yusuf Deng expressed appreciation for what had been achieved and warned against the consequences of any careless conduct.

A man who has just stumbled walks carefully. We are like a man who has just stumbled. We must know that we may stumble again. So, we must walk watching for what lies ahead. And what is ahead is that we might stumble again. So we must walk carefully to avoid the dangers.

Chief Arol Kacwol elaborates on the unpredictability of the situation and the need for both caution and patient observation.

If a man has a wound and he goes to the hospital, and the doctor gives him medicine with which to cure the wound, don't people wait and see what the medicine will do? Don't all the people watch the wound and see whether the medicine is working? In particular, you, the man who felt the pain of the wound, you will wait and see what the medicine will do. Even if other people may forget it, you will not forget it; you will watch the wound. And while you are watching to see the medicine work, you will have to protect the wound from flies or from anything that might injure it further. Even when it heals, the injured part becomes a scar.

Chief Stephen Thongkol likens regional autonomy to scraps of food thrown onto the ground for dogs and warns the South to be clever dogs and eat cautiously to avoid the trap.

This regional autonomy is like the situation in which scraps of food are thrown to the ground and dogs jump and start eating. A clever dog bites a piece of meat and looks around. But if a stupid dog goes in and eats without thinking about being attacked by something like a hyena, eating everything without worrying about what's going on around him, he may die. So we should eat what we have and look around.

In the words of Chief Makuei Bilkuei:

We, what do we hate, if this is what is decided? The Arab said, "You South, let us unite." Is that not what the Arab said? If you accept, you open one eye and close the other eye. Keep one eye closed. Let one eye speak with the Arab and let the other eye remain closed. Nimeri said to us that the country is one, that the black people have been given their own house. They have been given their wives to bear their children in their own house. Tomorrow we will meet in the field when we have borne our children in our little huts. But don't accept the breast.

By breast, Chief Makuei seems to imply that the Southerners are being allured and deceived by Northerners with superficial pleasures.

A woman, if she allows you to hold her breast, then she

has allowed you a lot more. If she allows you to touch
the breast, then she has allowed you to touch her groin,
and if she has allowed you to touch her groin, she has
allowed you to commit a wrong. Tomorrow, she will go
and confess that you have done this and that. Then you
will be killed. It is the vagina which causes troubles. It is
the breast which causes troubles. So, you today, now
that you people have held the breasts of a woman and
you have been attracted and attracted and are still being
attracted, you are all dying, holding the breast of the
Arab. You will all finish one by one, holding the breast.
He may even give you the groin of his woman. You will
touch the groin and then suddenly we will hear that
Mading is dead.

Among the elements of the problem that Chief Stephen
Thongkol predicts are the Northern traders in the South:

The evil will come from the traders, our traders here in
the South. Those are the people who will bring trouble.
Did you not see how they tried to kill Nimeri when they
heard that the police were taken away from the South?
God refused; God stopped them. They wanted to compli-
cate matters and they were caught. That is good. God
has saved us on that.

When we come to the question of the army—the army
which was supposed to combine South and North—there
is no problem. There were also the police and the prison
wardens and the traders. The police have gone and the
wardens have gone. What about this man who has remained here called the trader? What shall we do about
him?

Chief Ayeny Aleu considers unity to be a concession the
Southerners must make because they had not the power to
impose separation on the North. However, he sees the arrangement as temporary, and separation as both inevitable

and desirable, because of the bitterness and the chronic animosity the two sides have toward each other: "The things we have endured during these periods of destruction, they are things which make us look at each other with bad eyes. Even when we meet and we greet them, we greet them, but we are not really with them."

In answer to my question about what the war has meant in terms of the magnitude of destruction, Chief Ayeny said:

> What about the son of your own father who was installed in your father's place to be chief; didn't you hear that he was killed? The Arab has spoiled the country; he has completely destroyed our country. And this is the man; we say Nimeri is our brother. If Akuein has a brother, and his brother kills your people and he says, "I am your brother," would you accept that? Can we say, "This man, we will keep among us," when his brother has killed our own people?

Chief Ayeny sees five years as the cutoff point. After describing the suffering the South underwent during the civil war to demonstrate its vulnerability at the moment, he concluded with this:

> Even with these things, can I really say we will break it apart? How can we break the relationship? Where is the strength to do so?
>
> We are still one; we and the Northerners are still one. Let us spend these five years together. A child is born and he begins by lying down on his stomach. Then he thinks of it and turns to one side. Then he begins to crawl. Then he begins to raise his head and push himself up trying to walk. When he is able to walk, he will then begin to think. A man walks, thinking with his head, until his hair turns grey.
>
> Let us strengthen our position and begin to close the ways by which the Arabs have been subduing us. When

we have blocked those ways, we can then turn to them and say, "Now that we have become so educated, and now that we have become so able, how are we both going to fit into the South, you the Arabs and ourselves the Southerners? Can you not now move aside and give us room and freedom to look after our country?"

Chief Ayeny demonstrated his determined commitment to separation in his answer to the question: "What if Nimeri survives and the country proceeds well, if things go well between us and the North, if we enjoy full peace and relate to one another in an atmosphere of friendliness, what will happen?" This was his reply:

Again, I say that our years with the North will be five; they should just be five. As soon as they reach six, we should cut it off. Beyond that, our educated men should be numerous enough to run the South. They should then live alone and we live alone. Even if Nimeri survives, and we are living well, after five years, we should then tell Nimeri, "Thank you very much; you have kept us and you have benefited us. Now that the years have become five, please go back home and leave us alone; let us now be left alone to suffer by ourselves. If we should be hungry, we will go into the forest and look for wild fruits."

Chief Thon Wai opposes unity as dependence on the North and advocates separation marked by complementary cooperation between South and North.

These people want us to live in their hands, to be their people, feeding in their hands. That cannot be. Now that we have been given our small chance through autonomy, we will work with that little chance. We will exchange the things which each one of us will not do by himself. What is too difficult for me, I will call my brother and say, "This thing is too much for me." What is too much for them, they will call us and say, "This is too much for us."

But we will stay with some distance between us, because it cannot be otherwise. If we continue to mingle, who knows, the next day we will start tricking one another. And when it dawns, we may get into conflict and a war may again disrupt us. People will again die as they have died.

Chief Ayeny Aleu emphasizes the education and development of the South as prerequisites to a breakaway.

We have been given time for our children in schools to grow and learn. And if they grow up and become learned and unite hands with you, the Arab will say goodbye to us and leave us fully free. There will be no longer a war between us. They will simply say goodbye, and leave us alone to run our own affairs.

Chief Stephen Thongkol, also building his argument on the premise that the history of South-North relations is too bitter for unity to be meaningfully effected and peace permanently guaranteed, warns that clinging to the principle of unity could be hazardous.

If we are to stick together, because of the pains that we remember from the past there will be a problem. We will be slighted and there might be a fight one day. And the next fight will not leave us fat. We will suffer from it. All of us should do our best to prevent it because if there is a war it is going to affect us all.

As the words of Chief Ayeny indicate, some of the chiefs believe that the desired separation could be achieved peacefully and with mutual understanding if the South demonstrates sufficient strength, for which the unity of the South is an important prerequisite. But most of the chiefs foresee

that it will probably not be easy and that a war might erupt
again, either in the attempt by the North to oust Nimeri and
undo what he has done, or by the refusal of the North, including Nimeri, to ultimately recognize Southern independence. In the event of the former, Chief Ayeny pledged
support for Nimeri and, according to him, he communicated
that message to Nimeri personally in the following words:

> If you should think that you have solved the Southern
> problem and rest assured that the problem is ended,
> and something goes wrong with people working against
> you behind your back, remember that I am here right
> behind you. If there are people who go underground,
> we want to assure you, bull of our father, do not fear
> anything. We the Sudanese are brave people and even
> if we are only ten, we Southerners, we can do what we
> want to do. We will walk right into Khartoum. And we
> will finish in Khartoum. We will no longer finish in the
> region called the South. We will die in the middle of
> Khartoum. This time, it will be Khartoum that will be
> fought for and not the South. If anything should make
> you fall, then I assure you, even I, who is so grey with old
> age, I will walk on foot.

On the possibility of the North, including Nimeri, deciding
to deny the South eventual separation, the chiefs expressed
the Southern willingness (and indeed determination) to go
back to war. Chief Thon sees the struggle as one that is time-
less and can be continued through successive generations:

> Man is like a tree, the tree that grows from the earth;
> and man is like grass that grows from the earth. One
> group goes and another group grows. We chiefs used
> to think that our people were all destroyed, that no
> tribe would remain; but people do not disappear. Gener-
> ations die and other generations grow. People never

totally disappear. And the hand of the man who wants to kill all of us will eventually be tired.

While the sense of antagonism with the North is strongly felt and voiced as against the South, there is a universal desire for the consolidation of Southern unity which is generally agreed to be threatened by persistent tribalism. According to Deng Riny, speaking of Southerners in the interview with Chief Albino Akot:

> They are still having a lot of problems. Even if it is not too much, it is still there. It is not very open but it is there. People whisper and some people are beginning to whisper louder and louder. For instance, in Juba today you may hear some talk of tribalism: so and so has become this; this tribe has become this. Now they say, "The Dinka are the ones controlling our government; they have become the supreme power," and all that. This is common talk outside here that we have captured the country. So this is not something that can easily be resolved. But there is no way out; we have to push it slowly—slowly because we cannot force cooperation.

Chief Yusuf had this to say about the sensitive issue of Dinka leadership of the South:

> It is the Dinka today who have assumed the responsibility. They are the people doing the job. We hear it from different sources. But it is not official, nobody is saying it officially. When you hear something, you should sit and think together about it. Let the Dinka gather together with a leader and think at night and discuss the matter in the middle of the night. Do not sleep.

And in another context, Chief Yusuf pursued the point of how best the Dinka can reconcile the minority tribes through recognition and accommodation.

A stranger must be kept close to people. So, you, the
leaders, have to think hard as to what will win the non-
Dinka and bring them into the picture, bring them to
share with us. But if you start saying, "I have found my
job and I will bring my brother next to me and not this
stranger," that is when complaints will multiply and the
people who have been deprived, the groups which have
not been given a share, will get together and unite. They
will unite and destroy the system. It is work we should
put our hearts into and unite ourselves as one people.
What we are now facing is like a feud; people should
unite their hands and fight together. People who are
threatened by the same thing become relatives; they
unite and fight a common front.

According to Chief Giirdit, the issue of whether the South
will unite and remain united depends on how skillfully the
smaller tribes are accommodated by the larger tribes like the
Nilotics: "If you people do not give a good place to them in
your society, I suspect that one day they will break away."

Chief Yusuf Deng illustrates the importance of unity with
a tale.

According to the tale, a man had grown to be a very old
man. He called his seven children and brought seven
canes. Then he asked them one by one to take a cane
and break it. He asked the eldest son and he broke the
cane. Then he asked another and he broke the cane. That
way they all broke all the seven canes.

Then the father took seven pieces of canes and said to
the eldest son, "Break them." The son tried but could
not break them. They all tried but could not. Then he
said to them, "My sons, I'm old and about to die. If you
should separate and go your own individual ways, know
that you are doomed to a lonely death just as it was easy
for you to break individual canes. But if you unite, you

will be difficult to break. Any danger will find you difficult to harm."

Thus, while the peace settlement is deeply appreciated and viewed as nearly miraculous and while Nimeri is viewed as exceptionally wise in ending the civil war, the Dinka are acutely aware of the fragility of the arrangement, especially in view of the long-standing animosity that has marked the relations between the two sides of the country. As a result, they are rather skeptical about unity and some tend to value it only as an interim arrangement, pending eventual separation. In sharp contrast, Southern unity is advocated as one of the sources of strength that will ensure a Southern march ahead in terms of development or eventual separation. Thus, contrary to the optimism one might expect to result from the ideal manner in which the solution came about and the goodwill presently demonstrated by Northern leadership, the chiefs still view the future as bleak. However, despite their pessimism, they are allowing room for better alternatives which they vaguely characterize with a wait-and-see attitude. Theirs is the pessimism of a man who has suffered too much and who must no longer take anything for granted; he must now be convinced by deeds and not by ideals.

The facts of the current situation, however, tend to show that deeds are working toward consolidated unity. Naturally, one cannot be dogmatic about prediction, and the situation is complex enough for caution to be understandable, if not justified. However, the enthusiasm with which the South now supports the May Revolution and its leadership, though personified in Nimeri as an individual, and the fact that the present leadership is worthy of this support because of its bold stand for the rights of the South and the interests of the nation as a whole, would seem to indicate a significant breakthrough in the restructuring of the political process.

In order to get a more comprehensive view of the predict-

able future, the perspectives of the chiefs and elders should
be placed in the context not only of Northern determination
to maintain national unity, but also of Africa's commitment
to the preservation of the boundaries inherited from colonialism and the promotion of more inclusive concepts of regional
and continental unity. This commitment is not only en-
shrined in the Charter of the Organization of African Unity,
but is vigorously pursued individually and collectively by the
member states, nearly all of whom have conditions favoring
actual or potential separatist movements in their countries.
This position is reinforced through bilateral and multilateral
efforts, including institutional arrangements with international organizations. Seen in this broadened framework of
which the chiefs are naturally unaware, it is most unlikely,
if not impossible, that any local or national separatist movements in Africa will gain more than autonomous, at most
federal, recognition. The cases of the Province of Katanga in
what was then the Congo and of Biafra in Nigeria are glaring
examples of the African determination to maintain unity at
whatever cost and usually by full suppression of the separatist movement.

This means that whatever the preferred model of the
Dinka chiefs, a fundamental and overriding value has already
been placed on unity, and is indeed acknowledged by pivotal
elements within the national constitutive process, including
Southern leadership. The implication of this is that instead
of the simplistic South-North equation, a greater degree of
realism and a more complex appreciation of local, national,
and international dimensions have emerged and are likely to
crystallize even more with increasing political sophistication.
Whatever new and formidable problems and challenges this
emerging situation presents for the Sudan, the dynamics
inherent in the process are quite likely to blur, if not to
eliminate, the South-North dividing line in favor of consoli-

dated national unity. That the South and almost certainly
the North remain cautious and apprehensive about the future
should underscore the degree to which expounding and
observing appropriate bases for realizing this postulated and
predicted trend toward consolidated unity is vital. Failure
will not achieve any exclusive goals and can only be cata-
strophic beyond what the country has already suffered; and
that, the Dinka tell us, has been tantamount to the spoiling—
the destruction—of the world.

Development

An important feature of the postwar page of Sudanese
history is the striking acceptance of, indeed demand for,
development which is being displayed throughout the country, even by traditional peoples who have generally been
known for their resistance to change. In this, the Dinka constitute a remarkable example, for, contrary to what has
always been assumed about their conservatism, the reality
of their modern world as reflected in the accounts of the
chiefs demonstrates a surprising commitment to, and a cry
for, accelerated development. Indeed, the success of regional
autonomy for the South is seen as directly dependent on
the degree to which the South will succeed in development.
This shift calls for a closer look at the roots of the alleged
conservatism of the Dinka in order to better appreciate the
recent changes in their outlook.

Dinka ethnocentrism is essentially implicit in their procreational orientation and agnatic continuity. Pride in their
ancestors and all their ways is a necessary condition to their
continued veneration. The system is therefore essentially
conservative and, while not resistant to change, is selective
and restrained; outside elements are adopted and assimilated
to reinforce, rather than to alter, the preexisting system.
This feature is common to all Nilotics, especially the Nuer

and to a lesser extent the Shilluk, and has been widely observed and written about. In his book, *The Christian Church in Post-War Sudan,* Trimingham observed in 1949 :

> One of the determinants of the rapid or slow spread of Christianity in the South has been provided by the contrast between semi-nomadic cattle-breeding Nilotic tribes (Shilluk, Nuer and Dinka) and the settled agriculturists. The life of the former is bound up with a cow economy, this animal being a veritable god. They are intensely conservative and very proud of their civilization.[1]

Audrey Butt also wrote of the Nilotics:

> They consider their country the best in the world and everyone inferior to themselves. For this reason they . . . scorn European and Arab culture. . . . . Their attitude toward any authority that would coerce them is one of touchiness, pride, and reckless hatred of submission. They are self-reliant; brave fighters, turbulent and aggressive, and are extremely conservative in their aversion to innovation and interference.[2]

But as I have already indicated, Nilotic conservatism has been grossly exaggerated. It has now become apparent that throughout earlier historical phases they rejected what they considered not worth adopting and selected what they considered desirable, assimilating it into their own culture to the point where it eventually lost its foreign character.

As I have argued elsewhere, Nilotic resistance to change was indeed aggravated by the colonial policies which kept the tribes isolated and tried to preserve traditional cultures. As a result of intensive cross-cultural interaction and of

1. John S. Trimingham, *The Christian Church in Post-War Sudan* (London and New York, World Dominion Press, 1949), p. 34.
2. Audrey Butt, *The Nilotes of the Anglo-Egyptian Sudan and Uganda* (London, International African Institute, 1952), p. 41.

modern education, the process of selection has been accelerated and indeed revolutionized so much that the Nilotics
have demonstrated and are demonstrating more adaptability
to change than could ever have been predicted only two
decades ago.

This process has led to, and is now catalyzed by, the
Dinka realization that there can be, and indeed is, much in
the ways of others which by far excels that of the Dinka,
at least in certain respects, and would be enriching for the
Dinka to adopt. So great has the impact of this realization
been that the Dinka are becoming at times self-degrading in
the face of the superiority of foreign skills and technology.
One can now say that ethnocentrism and self-exaltation in
defense of tradition go side by side with admissions of
deprivation and, to some extent, of the technological inferiority of Dinka traditional society. The greater the realization
of the latter, the stronger the defense mechanisms of the
former. The external threats now facing the Dinka, the
negative self-image which has emerged with the impact
of external factors, and the counter-myths of self-glorifica-
tion in defense of the threatened traditions emerge strongly
in the accounts of the interviewed chiefs and elders.

Advocating a degree of separate existence between the
North and the South in order to avoid the possibility of
further friction and conflict, Chief Thon Wai said:

> War will finish our people. It kills the man at home, the
> man who knows nothing.
>   The ordinary men in the tribe and their chiefs are like
> sheep. A man who is not educated and who does not
> know what is said between nations is ignorant; he is like
> cattle and like sheep. If a man drives sheep and cattle
> into the river, they may drown. Sheep may kill them-
> selves and cattle too may kill themselves. An educated
> man, if driven, knows what to do. He may escape at the
> right time. If there is a rope around his neck, he may be

able to loosen himself from it, but not a man who is not educated. Most of our people in the South are not educated.

There may, of course, be a linkage between the objectives of the revolution and the chiefs' commitment to development, but there is also another facet to it. It is now generally recognized that the trend is away from such traditional institutions as chieftainship. The present socialist revolution in the Sudan makes this quite clear. Indeed, while chieftainship in the South has been allowed to continue because of the degree of traditionalism still pertaining there, the institution has been abolished in the North. This has created in the Southern chiefs a degree of insecurity; they must therefore prove both subjectively and objectively that they are capable of bridging the gap between their traditionalism and the demands of development, or else remain anachronistic or even be dismissed. It is the interplay of these subjective and objective factors in their search for relevancy and self-assertiveness that makes the chiefs so preoccupied with the issue of development, some to the point of obsession.

According to Chief Thon Wai:

> What has been given to us today, let us work for with strength: let the commissioner work with strength; let the inspector work with strength; let the officers work with strength; let the chiefs work with strength. If the commissioner is working well, let him be promoted; if an inspector works well, let his powers be increased; if a chief works well, let his powers be increased; if a retainer works well, give him power; every chief of any section who does well, give him recognition. A man who does not know how to work, let him be told, "Brother, stop." Let him stand still like water in a pool which does not flow with the current. A man who works, let him be given the power of the flowing river. He is like the

waters of a running river. A man who does not know how to work, let him be seated; let him be put in a pool where he cannot swim, where the water does not run, where he will remain seated and idle. Let him be in stagnant water, the water which does not go forward or backward. This is what we have to say, we Southerners and Northerners.

Chief Yusuf Deng speaks of the sacrifices that must now be made to guarantee a happier future in a truly independent South, where people will have laid their own foundation and built their own house.

You should stop eating and stop wearing clean clothes and do work. Eat afterwards in the days ahead. When the summer comes, let one not walk leisurely. Let a person take a hoe and wear his old clothes. Let him spend the summer in his old clothes. In the winter, when he has cultivated his crops, and his crops have ripened, and he has reaped them and threshed them and sold them, that's the day when he will wear his good clothes. So, consider this the summer. Let us wait for the winter and let us work in the meantime. Even if it takes two years or five years, let us work. And let us find the winter before five years pass. It is better that badness comes first to be followed by goodness. But if goodness comes before badness, then it is not good. Badness is good when you go through it looking forward to goodness. But we have to work for that goodness.

According to Chief Thon Wai:

That day, when we all finish with death, the land will remain with our children. And it will remain with the children of our children. The children of our children will find a world that is theirs, and our children are the ones who will inherit from us. We have to leave them in a cleared field. And that day when our grandchildren come, they too will find a cleared field. The sun will shine on them and the moon will shine on them. Nothing will trouble them. They will remain on a clear plain—a place where no scrubs will pierce their feet and no thorns will hurt their faces and nothing wrong will happen to them; nothing like the things we are now experiencing.

Speaking of the reservations of most Northerners about the peace settlement, Chief Yusuf stresses the point that the South is on trial and must prove itself worthy of autonomy.

So, let us know that we are being followed and observed, now that the President has reversed the trend. Some of his own brothers do not want us to have what he has given us. Even the people who recently tried to do what they tried to do, it was because the leader had said that he would give the South her rights. If it is said that we do not deserve what has been given us, but it is given to us so that it is in our hands, then we must now earn it with work. That is the only way we can compensate ourselves. That is how we can compensate ourselves for our men who died in the conflict. We can only compensate ourselves for them with our own work.

Like most Southerners today, Chief Yusuf is particularly concerned about what might go wrong to disrupt the peace and he sees the remedy in preoccupation with work, each in his own specialized role.

A very small thing that might go wrong is what we want to guard against. Each man has his own ways and his own work given to him. That is what he can do. . . . It is like cultivating a field. When you work in the field during the season of cultivation, there is a man who leaves very early from the field and there is a man who spends the whole day working in the field until nightfall. The man who works late is seen by others and by those who work late too. Building a country is like building a house. There are some people who will build their walls with big bricks, others who build with mud. There are people who are good in thatching. We should filter away those people who will not build our huts well.

According to Chief Stephen Thongkol:

What we are going into now are big matters. We should plan carefully so that we get good doctors, so that we improve our roads, so that we improve our education. We must improve our cultivation so that if hunger comes we don't have to depend on the North. Now we do have to depend on the North if hunger comes. Our cleverness will depend on growing our food. Then we have to get lorries for transportation and do many other things.

Chief Ayeny Aleu addressed himself to the prevention and cure of human and animal diseases: "We have no medicine for cattle and for people. We asked for medicine, and what did we get? Only aspirin for headaches. . . . Our cattle are dying; they are being exterminated by disease and there is no medicine for them; and there is no medicine for people." Chief Ayeny continued to list more of the services he considered urgently needed in the South:

Another thing, now that it is said that our country is back in order, where are the tractors? Where are the machines for cultivating the fields? They have not yet come. And thirst, we are still suffering from thirst; we are truly suffering. Leave this simple thing called money, the kind of thing that is given for salaries. I am not talking about that.

Another thing, a dam has been built in Khashim el Girba. If that were made here in our country, water would flow to dry areas. A machine should be brought

to the South to do these things. It should be known
that the South has now begun to be put back into good
condition.

Yet another thing, talk to us about schools; let us
build schools for our children to learn. That is what will
enter our heads. If a man has five children or has ten
children, let them be sent to school. Some will fail and
become the servants in towns; others will fail and come
back home. They will be sent to take care of cattle.

Chief Ayeny gives an example of a confrontation which
was very common during the initial stages of Dinka introduction to modern education:

I have seven children of my own and I have sent them
all to school.

Women cried and I beat them into silence. I said to
them, "So it is you women who are keeping us behind
by refusing to send your children to school. You are
keeping the South behind. These are the cattle; it is we
who looked for them, not the children; why should
they be kept behind because of the cattle that we are
responsible for? No one is going to force them to stay
and take care of cattle. Let them go. Their own strength
will come back in the future."

Chief Ayeny even considers adult education essential for the
proper care of cattle, a task which has traditionally been used
to justify not sending boys to school.

Chief Thon Wai had this to say on the theme of education,
agriculture, marketing, and health services:

Let all the chiefs speak about opening schools. Let them
speak about cultivating crops. Crops provide food as well
as products for sale in the market. Everything begins
with the market. It provides many things so that a man
no longer needs to travel far to the distant towns. Grain

will be cultivated and traded to provide cash which can be used for developing the country. It will also be used for building schools.

Diseases are on the increase. There is a disease called kalazaar which is killing people and a disease which causes headaches. There are diseases which did not exist at the time of our grandfathers. And what brought them? It is because those foreigners came and other foreigners came and people intermingled. All the diseases which were absent are now amidst us. For these we need hospitals.

And with what money will they be built? They will be built with the money of the people. The chief must collect the money. The chief must establish cooperatives. The chief must hold meetings and ask his people to build houses and then say to the government, "We want a doctor to be brought." He would give his letter of request to the Commissioner.

On the same theme of self-help, Chief Makuei Bilkuei had this to say:

Let me tell you what we have to do to improve ourselves. This wound you see on my hands is a wound from making roads. Ever since the government came my people have been building their own roads. I have always made the roads. Money has never come into my tribe to be paid for working on the roads. The cattle at home are all in your hands. Many of the things in the tribe are in your hands to show us what we can do with them. I collected money before I left and put it into a box. I came and asked, hoping that the government would give me a truck to go and build my own area by myself. That's all I want. I just want a truck and I have the money. I don't want any help. I want a car and I want tools. I want axes. I want to build schools and I want to build hospitals. Those are all the things I am asking from you. And we

need the thing that cultivates the ground for crops.
When we cultivate the crops, part of it will be sold and
part of it will be eaten.

Struggling over power is viewed as detracting from the main
objective of reconstruction and development and is con-
demned. In the words of Chief Ayeny Aleu:

People are fighting, saying, "Well, are you going to make
the son of Deng the head of all of us? What about I, son
of so and so and what about him, the son of so and so?"
That way, the affairs of the country get spoiled and
the country is held back. If only one were left alone,
observed, and given time to try to do something for the
country, it would be much better. If you do wrong
things, then people can come and say, "This is wrong;
this is the way to do it," and you go on doing it. True, we
have held our country, but it will not go ahead, because
the eyes of the people are focused on positions of power.

Chief Thon Wai had this to say on the issue of a power
struggle:

Let us put all our hearts into the advancement of our
country and leave the struggle for power to be a later
issue. If you find a leader among yourselves, a man who
has a good head and knows the work and a man who looks
ahead, a man who teaches people to cultivate and teaches
them to say good words, a man who will say, "Let us build
our country and put our country in order," give that man
power and let it be known that he has been placed in the
lead.

Chief Yusuf Deng warns against arrogance and the self-
delusion that one knows how to do things and therefore
does not need to learn or try harder.

We should work hard knowing that there are things that

may prove too much for us. If a man says, "I am able to do all things," then that man is a failure. If a man works hard and recognizes that some things may be difficult for him, that man will succeed and proceed ahead. It is what you are sure you can do which defeats you. You will lie down thinking you are so able that you cease to work.

For Chief Yusuf, however, productive modesty should not be confused with ineptness and a feeling of inadequacy, which he rejects as retarding progress.

If you people do not think and open your eyes and think of yourselves as good people and not think of yourselves as people who are bad, if you people with power think that you are not able to do the best for your country, then I think our work will not go well; our work will stray from its path.

According to Chief Yusuf, there are able people in the South to do what needs to be done and it was indeed their being denied their rightful positions which provoked the conflict.

Today, we have able people, people who are highly suited for responsible positions. If they are well distributed, we can say that we have fared well. That was what brought us into conflict.

As for writing, it is all one. Writing in English is now known to our people, and writing in Arabic is also known to our people. There is no difference in writing. What is it therefore that makes people believe that we may not be able to do the job when education is all one? The education of a university boy from the North and the education of a university boy from the South are not different. The difference only comes with the individual's ability to think. There will be a good-thinking

boy in the South and a good-thinking boy in the North.
There are no essential differences.

Despite the call for unity, cooperation, and harmonious
relations, recognition of individual merits or demerits implies
constant appraisal and a tension in social relations which, at
least according to Chief Yusuf Deng, is essential for achievement and development.

> Do not take pride that you have been blessed with posi-
> tions. Don't say that you have been given your dish of
> food and that you may now eat laughing. No, eat quar-
> reling; yes, eat quarreling. A man who works well you
> should recognize. But don't say that you may now laugh.
> This has been given to you, but when you are given a
> good thing, eat it knowing that you might miss it one
> day. If you eat with enjoyment, not wondering whether
> you will always have it, only chance will keep it with
> you. It is the truth which remains; a lie is swept away.
> Truth cannot be removed. A land governed by truth
> will continue.

And according to Chief Thon Wai, again linking development with the fundamental value of the Dinka—procreation:

> There will be a separation determined by work. The
> country will separate not by hatred but by strength of
> work. If we are strong enough we will hold our own
> government by our hands. Even if we are dead, it will
> remain with our children—the children we will bear. Even
> those children in their wombs today, when the baby is
> born, the father will have much to say to that child. He
> will say, "The day the country came back to peace, it
> happened this way and that way and this way and that
> way." All that will remain with the child.

So radical have the Dinka become in their commitment to

development that according to the chiefs' accounts, there is
now a striking willingness to change the traditional Dinka
ways, including their belief in the aesthetic and social value
of cattle, which is considered to be inconsistent with development. According to Chief Makuei Bilkuei:

> When I was at home I told all my people, "The North
> burned down our villages during the war. Everything is
> now gone. The rebels have broken down the tribe. So,
> what we have to do is this: you contribute money, each
> man five pounds, five pounds." I took all that and left
> it at home. I told them, "You people are going to re-
> main behind. I want an axe and I want a truck. When I
> come back from Juba, I want the cattle to be made use
> of. Cattle have become ill and the government has said
> they are to be collected as taxes. So I think that we
> have to make use of our cattle." That is being done
> now while I am away.

Chief Ayeny Aleu sees the challenge of development in
terms of comparison with the North.

> I myself have traveled and have gone as far as Kosti, and I
> have gone as far as Port Sudan; I have gone as far as
> Shendi, and I have gone as far as Kassala. I have seen how
> well built the North is. And it is not that we do not have
> the means to do the same; we have a lot of cattle in
> the South and we have a lot of sheep and goats and we
> have chickens.
>   If we are given our country, we can abandon our cattle
> and put everything into what will help our country to
> go ahead. We will surrender our sheep and goats and
> we will surrender our chickens. Are these not the things
> which turn into money with which a country can be
> built? If we sell them, won't we get enough cash to help
> build our country? That's what we should do.

So revolutionary was Chief Ayeny Aleu that he opposed high bridewealth:

> I, myself, I spoke to my own people. I said, "This costly marriage of the Dinka in which a hundred cows must be paid, I have forbidden it; I have forbidden it entirely. And if any man breaks my order, he will see my punishment. No girl, whatever she is, should be married for more than ten and at the very most twenty cows. Marriage will stop at twenty cows. What is it that brings a hundred cows into marriage?"

Chief Makuei even foresaw a time when the Dinka would no longer marry with cattle:

> You see, cattle are now in a predicament. There is illness, there's marriage, there is taxation, there are fines; all fall on cattle. So, you see, one day the Dinka will accept something other than marriage with cattle. They will accept it. Cattle have become scarce and they are increasingly becoming more scarce. For instance, girls who have not been married yet, they wait for marriage until they must give up and do something else because of lack of cattle. You see, one day people may even decide to give breasts away and say, "So and so, take the girl and beget children with her," without any question of paying cattle for marriage.

So drastic is the change in Dinka economics that instead of relying on or taking pride in wealth accruing through such kinship sources as bridewealth, it is now fashionable to value self-acquired wealth above that which automatically accrues from status. As Chief Ayeny conveys, the father's function is increasingly becoming viewed as one of helping his child, notably through education, to acquire the necessary skills to stand on his own feet and acquire his independent wealth or means.

I have a son in Rumbek Secondary School. I told him, "In case it ever enters your head to say, 'My father has wealth,' let me tell you, they are not your cattle; these are my cattle with your mother. You have never gone to look for cattle. If you do not make your own wealth, and become a man by your strength, I am not near you; we are not to be relatives. If that happens, don't consider me your father.

The first of his three years [he is now in his third year] I collected a lot of bulls and gave them to him to sell. He sold them and flew by plane. Then he came back. The second year, I again gave him cattle and said, "Drive them and sell them." I said, "Never mind the cattle; let us sell them; let us kill them; but what you will do with what we are giving you, I will watch with my eyes."

While the chiefs emphasize self-reliance and advocate an end to dependency on the North, they expect assistance from the Northerners to help them stand on their own, and such assistance is not viewed as charity but as brotherly support or compensation for past wrongs. Chief Yusuf Deng expressed the former theory thus:

Our situation with the North is that of a man whose brother is obliged to help him because his crops have not yet ripened. We also say that when a man's sister is married, he must give his brother a share in the bride-wealth. He is your brother. You were born of the same person. Even if he has no sister of his own, you must give him a share of your sister's bridewealth. If a man refuses to give a share to his brother, that brother is entitled to come to court and say, "So and so has refused to give me a share in his sister's bridewealth." He will be forced to give the share. Why? Because they are one.

In a combined theory of compensation and brotherly

sharing of resources, Chief Yusuf evaluates Nimeri's generous
attitude toward the South in the following words:

> He has known the debt owed to us, the debt of our
> destroyed people; our people who have died by thirst;
> our people who have died at the hands of their own
> brothers, since we were made to kill one another, our
> people who have died in his hands, the hands of our
> brother in the North who, when he was told that the
> rebels had passed through a cattle-camp, would not
> follow those who had gone but would kill the people who
> had remained.

There is however an acute sense of urgency behind what
the South demands from itself and from its supporters and
debtors. Returning to the theme of delayed reaction cited
earlier, Chief Thon said:

> If there is a chance of what goes wrong being put right,
> it should be finished in that one day so that the person
> concerned may return to his home and the other man
> remain in his home! Instead, what we hear is "tomor-
> row," "tomorrow," "tomorrow." "Tomorrow" brings
> quarrels. I may leave and go to sit in my house, disap-
> pointed. I may never return. So now that we have taken
> control of our country, let us not adopt "tomorrow,"
> we the children of the land.

The contribution demanded from the individual is extreme-
ly high. In the words of Chief Thon Wai:

> What we call the country is put in order by a man who
> does not sleep. A man who sleeps is not a man; he is bad.
> But a man who stands up and works hard and knows the
> work of the morning and the night, he makes night and
> day one thing; he is a good man. He is a man who helps
> his people.

Thus, whether it is a manifestation of characteristics in the Dinka, hitherto hidden by their isolationism, or the result of the impact of the civil war, or simply an adaptability to the circumstances they now live in, the Dinka are demonstrating a degree of commitment to development that will surprise the observers of the 1950s and even later commentators. Whichever is the explanation, their preoccupation with development is conceptually linked with their desire for self-liberation from all the bondages they have experienced, especially under the post-colonial period of domestic hostilities. Development thus becomes an envisaged weapon against a feared return to the hostilities that are now gone but continue to haunt the Dinka, not only in the psychic world of the survivors but also in the rationalized possibilities of the future. Development is therefore both an objective pursuit and a subjective resort—a material and moral defense against apprehensions.

Integration

Earlier, I analyzed the actual functioning of autonomy in the South as involving a paradoxical process in which the central authorities exercise a centrifugal force which tends to pull regional participation into the center through a form of decision-making osmosis, while the regional authorities tend to exercise these centrally controlled decisions in an atmosphere of flamboyant enjoyment of what appears to be a loose autonomy, almost approximating independence within unity. We have also seen that the very labels used, namely the intensified cry not only for the "desired" but also the allegedly "achieved" unity, are phenomena of a paradoxical nature in view of the fact that they are predicated on an autonomous settlement. I have also pointed out that it is indeed the delicate balances posed by these paradoxes that make the louder crying of unity slogans all the more functional and necessary. All these—the osmosis of central control, the enclave of regional independence within unity, the anomalies of unity in diversity, and the functional corrections implicit in the labels—are part of a subtle generic process, the inner logic of which is not necessarily clear to most Sudanese, including some leaders. From a national conceptual point of view, we can speculate that the process might end in either of the opposed alternatives now seemingly harmonized in the functional system of paradoxes; consolidated unity and integration or continued diversification and possible drifting apart.

The first line of thought is that the political osmosis, which is nationally centered, could and quite likely will result in an integration of elements that are nationally based, if not clearly conceived. And I am thinking not only of the political process but also of the more subtle cultural, social, and psychological processes. This means that the dominant elements in the outcome of national interaction, interdependence, and integration will be overtly Northern. I say "overtly" because the outcome of any interaction can never reflect solely either of the interacting principals. There is always a give and take and the proportions are never easily gaugeable. After all, it is now well established that the North is both African and Arab, and we can never be sure of the proportions. At least we know that the African proportion is far greater than was, and is still, acknowledged. "Overtly" therefore refers to the manifest, the acknowledged, the glorified, even when that may mask the real. So the predicted outcome of integration between South and North could be equitably shared in its constituent elements but inequitably shared in its labels of outward characterization. This alternative model would be quite comparable to the way Afro-Arab integration was brought about in the Northern Sudan.

Another possibility within the integrating trends is that the process and the outcome could reflect more of the hitherto denied side of the North and, of course, the South, which is more typically Sudanese—that is to say African, Afro-Arab, or simply and preferably "Sudanese." This is essentially what one would have predicted for the Sudan prior to the October war and its repercussions on the world scene. Previously the Sudanese searching for his true identity had been excavating the buried elements of his national character, which implied a degree of qualification of his Arabism and Islamic adherence in favor of his other, hitherto overshadowed, components. The outcome would have been a well-balanced view of the indigenous Afro-Christian-Arab-Islamic identity, more easily summarized as "Sudanese." Foreign policymakers could then use in international relations either of these elements or both, according to the context, for positive purposes in national, regional, or global interests, without blurring self-identity and national unity. The recent elevation of the Arab image on the global scene poses more complicating and complex choices for the Sudanese. I believe the predictable process continues, but the evolution toward a uniting national identity is faced with greater political and intellectual challenges in trying to bridge all the variables in a more sophisticated and globally conscious way than was the case a few years ago.

That the more equitable model is not only a Southern postulate, but an objective shared by progressive elements in the North as a sound basis for an enriched and unifying Sudanese identity, is reflected in these lines from the poem of Salah Ahmad Ibrahim which I referred to earlier:

> The flute is smashed but some of its sweetest
>   melodies are still swimming in the air
> I hear it with the ear of Walt Whitman saying
> May you live as brothers despite everything in
>   full brotherhood

Filling with love this big compound, this big
   homeland.
Its echoes are rolling in my blood
O ye garden of various flowers
In you I smell the aromas of a beautiful future
Where everybody is embracing the other
The way the tranquil White Nile and the vigorous
Blue Nile are flowing into each other in the
   confluence
And when they came together, and all of them . . .
Arabs, Bija, Nuba, Fajalo, Barya, Barta, Bango,
   Zagawa, Ambararu, Ingasana, Dinka, Tabula,
   Ashuli, Nuer, Masalit, Anuak, Latuka and others
   and more others
Coming to the festival with everyone present
But with jubilance and much self-confidence and pride
   his small thing . . .
Let us think together, Malual.[3]

The negative alternative could be to emphasize the divergent elements of identity and thus generate a political evolution toward political and cultural separatism and disintegration. The increasing trend toward wider national, regional, and international identification would tend to foreclose this alternative; yet the countercurrent of cultural, ethnic, or racial self-assertiveness, which implies fissions alongside fusions, is a paradoxical reality of our time and could simply mean plunging the country back into a destructive conflict that would not advance either separatism or imposed unity. The accounts of the chiefs in the interviews are less complex and less subtle than the process I have attempted to analyze. Some chiefs are experienced and wise enough to admit that the future is beyond their cognition and therefore prediction. Chief Arol Kacwol, arguing against

3. *Ghadhbat Al-Hababai*, p. 69–70.

prediction, conceives the future as having passed into the hands of the younger generations.

> When you had conflict with those people in the North, did you know it beforehand? Did you read about it in the books? Were you not all surprised when war suddenly came? So, you see, what you are asking me, I cannot answer beforehand. It will be for you people to live in it and to hear it and then to see how it works. We, your fathers, have now gone far ahead. We are now flying into a different world. You managed to solve your own big problems.
>
> It will be for you to share with your brothers in the North and to see how your share goes in the years to come. It is not something about which you can ask your fathers any more. Our stories are gone. New stories will now begin with you. The ancient stories you were asking us about have had their turn. The time has now come for your own stories to begin. So, instead of us being the story-tellers, it is now for you to be the story-tellers. It is also for you to bear your children for the stories you are now about to tell.

And in a later context, when I continued to press the question of the future upon him, he went on to say:

> How can I really tell? Here we are, at the moment we are united. In the past did we not call the white men, the English, "strangers" in this country? Did we not call them "strangers?" But when they left and we remained in our country, did things go well between us and the Arabs? Did we not have our own problems? Did problems not arise, especially between you, our educated sons, and the Northerners? And did that not bring death to our people? . . .
>
> So, the question you asked me, it is not really for you people to ask us that question. The question of how

people who are not relatives can live together and improve their relationship, all that is with you and not
with us. It is you people who know the good things that
will come out of this. And it is you people who know
what may go wrong in it. It is also you people who will
see what is right and what is wrong. It is for you to see
whether we are really going to be brothers or not.

For most, the wounds of the past are too painful for integration to be predicted, let alone postulated. We have already
heard views which suggest marking time and breaking away
at the opportune time. We have also heard views that allow
room for observation, but are essentially skeptical of the
durability of unity; they therefore predict an eventual
separation. Bulabek Malith is a good example of those who
are too bitter to conceive of the possibility of integration
and his reasons are based on the past experience of the
Dinka.

Mading, what you have asked is true. We who are sitting
here are elders. We know the ancient behavior of the
Arabs. Pagwot knows it, Biong knows it, and even though
I am younger, I have also seen it. Even if people become
really equal and the South gets educated and has full
freedom, the way elders like us see it in their hearts, it
seems that they will one day separate. The Northerner is
a person you cannot say will one day mix with the
Southerner to the point where the blood of the Arab will
become one. . . .

The things the Arab has done in our country, including
things which we have been told about by our elders, are
many. A man called Kergaak Piyin, an elder with whom
we used to sit, used to tell us the stories of our country's
destruction. He said, "Children, as I sit here, I wish that
any future destruction of the country does not find me
alive. Arabs are bad. Before they kill you, they cut your

muscles to make you an invalid who cannot walk; they put stone grinders on your hands and ask you to grind grain and then come from behind to prick your testicles; they put a thorn on the tip of a stick and give it to a small child to prick your testicles as you grind the grain. I hope any other destruction of the country does not find me alive." This was said by an old man called Kergaak.

As we sit here today, we elders, we have witnessed the destruction of the country. Some people died in this destruction. Some people survived until the country came back to peace. We have seen quite something of those things elders used to say about destruction. Our muscles have not been cut and our testicles have not been pricked, but something as painful as the pricking of testicles we have seen.

According to Chief Albino Akot, even though the issue of the future is difficult to determine, there is too much cultural diversity for integration between the South and the North to be effectively realized.

For the North and South to mix, so that they become one people, a people with one language and one religion, this is a very difficult question. During the political period, the government used to say that the South and North are one people. In terms of geographical boundaries in which it is said that the Sudan comprises this and that area, it is one. But we used to say that the people inside this country were not one people. They cannot be one people. Why? Because there are no common ways behind them, no social contacts between them, and no common culture between them.

Chief Akot is by no means in the minority because, for many, the impediments to integration are rooted in the profundity of the differences between the Southerners and the

Northerners. Asked what he thought would be the result of the interaction between Southerners and Northerners, now that the war is over, and whether he thought they could mix to form one single people, neither Arab nor Dinka, Northern nor Southern, just Sudanese, Chief Giirdit replied categorically that it could not be, but speculated on a form of continued unity in diversity.

> It cannot happen. I don't see how it could happen. You may live in peace, but that you will intermarry and mix to be one people, I cannot see. It would be very difficult. Perhaps if you, the Dinka, abandon cattle and all your ways, maybe it could happen. But I don't see how it will happen. You will live together, but there will be South and North. Even living together is only possible if you people handle the situation well. There are many people who appear to be one, but inside them they remain two. I think that is how you will live. A man has only one head and one neck, but he has two legs to stand on.

Chief Makuei Bilkuei sees obstacles in the Arab religious and cultural ethnocentrism, scorn for the Dinka ways, and desire to integrate with the South on the basis of Northern cultural identity. On the issue of Arabs eating only the meat of an animal slaughtered in the Islamic fashion and rejecting the meat of an animal slaughtered the Dinka way as "impure," he said:

> Here, I slaughter a bull and I call him to share my meat. I say, "Let us share our meat." But he refuses the meat I slaughter because he says it is not slaughtered in a Muslim way. If he cannot accept the way I slaughter my meat, how can we be relatives? Why does he despise our food? So, let us eat our meat alone. When we can share our meat with them, then we may be relatives.

Chief Makuei sees in this practice a combination of spiritual and racial elements of Arab character which he views as essentially different from those of the Southerner:

> Why: they insult us, they combine contempt for our black skin with pride in their religion. As for us, we have our own ancestors and our own spirits; the spirits of the Rek, the spirits of the Twic, we have not combined our spirits with their spirits. The spirit of the black man is different. Our spirit has not combined with theirs.
>
> You people are given this small thing and this small thing, while the Arabs keep their big things like their girls. And you are the soap with which we wash our things; you are our soap. Why don't we promote our own ways? Why do we take their ways without our own plan? What have you people done to promote our own ways with the Arabs?

But while speaking of the willingness to unite and integrate on the basis of mutual equality, Chief Makuei is as contemptuous of Northern culture as he alleges they are of Southern culture. This is strikingly apparent in his explanation of his ignorance of Arabic language: "God has forbidden me to speak Arabic. I asked God, 'Why don't I speak Arabic?' and He said, 'If you speak Arabic, you will turn into a bad man.' I said, 'There is something good in Arabic!' And he said, 'No, there is nothing good in it!'"

Chief Pagwot Deng, referring to past hostilities between the North and the South and the present inclusion of the Arab and the Dinka in one nation as a British imposition, proceeds to postulate a concept of diversified unity similar to that of Giirdit, a relationship with a recognition of the essential differences. Like Chief Makuei, Pagwot also holds a contemptuous view of the Arab character. "Their way is their way, and our way is our way. We are black people; we are not part of the Arabs."

It must be borne in mind that Chief Pagwot was speaking at

a time when the situation in Abyei was still precarious, if not in a turmoil. So bitter were the Ngok then that even such widely known cross-cultural phenomena as the adoption of the concept of the Mahdi in Dinka religion, which indicates a degree of cross-cultural integration, was explained away if not denied. According to Pagwot, answering my inquiry on the matter:

> What you were asking about that song, the song, "Mahdi, son of Deng Acuk," it was a man of the Rek who composed it and he was a religious man. If he was praising Mahdi, it was because people were afraid of Mahdi, as the Arabs would go and capture Rek children; that was just praise of a man who was feared. What will ever change this behavior? When people were praising the Mahdi, did anything change? Were people not made slaves in the Mahdi's own house? Were there no fences made for slaves in the Mahdi family?

Chief Biong Mijak stressed the point even more:

> This issue, the song "Mahdi, son of Deng Acuk," it was a man of God who composed it. He was simply possessed by the spirit. But what he called "Acuk" [literally black ants] are black people. He talked about black people whom he called Acuk. It was not the Arabs he was praising He just brought in the Mahdi. If the Arabs wrote it down otherwise, it is a lie; it is not our story.

It will also be recalled from earlier quotes that Biong Mijak, like Makuei Bilkuei, urged his educated men to defend their ways against Arab encroachment, arguing that integration would mean disregarding the differences which God created in men and would therefore be essentially offensive to God.

The burning issue in integration is intermarriage, which many consider the true means to mutual assimilation into an equitable identity. The advice of the British as reported by Bulabek Malith reveals a view widely shared by the Dinka.

The English said, "I doubt that you will live well with the Arabs unless they can marry your daughters and you marry their daughters, so that a man has maternal uncles and has cousins here. That is how you will become relatives. But if you do not intermarry, your feud will never end and you will be ill-treated by them."

According to Chief Arol Kacwol, intermarriage establishes an affinity which bridges any differences and removes any hostilities the parties might have had between them prior to their intermarriage. Arol does not directly comment on the prospects of intermarriage between the North and South, although he builds his argument on the relationship that now exists between them.

Even if a man were a slave or descended from a slave, and he marries into a family, he becomes a relative—he becomes a member of the family. Even our brothers who were taken away as slaves, by now they have probably found their circles and have combined with other peoples to create their own kinships. So, if a man has secured a wife, it is for him to bear his own blood and to bear the blood of his wife's kin.

When that happens, whatever there is between people should no longer be allowed to be like what we have just gone through between us and the Northerners. That war is now ended. The troubles we had were the troubles of peoples who were not related. Relationship kills those troubles and begins the new way of kinship.

According to Chief Albino Akot, who views the function of mixed marriage in much the same way as the English administrator who spoke to the Ngok, the class factor figures prominently in the Northern attitude against intermarrying with the Southerners.

If they really wished the South to become one country with the North without any differences to show that this is a Southerner and this a Northerner, the first thing they should have done was to encourage intermarriage. The South and the North would have intermarried. Each person would have a maternal uncle in the North and the other person would have a maternal uncle in the South. They would mix. There would be no problem today.

Chief Albino Akot also comments on the religious factor behind the opposition of some Northerners to mixed marriage.

Religion is used by some Arabs who are fanatic, and they like that very much. When we argue with them and say, "How can you marry my daughter and I do not marry your daughter?," they will tell us that it is because of religion.

And we say, "If it is religion, why do you marry my daughter even if she has a different religion?"

And they say, "Yes, I can marry her according to my religion but my religion does not allow us to give you our daughters."

"Why?"

"Because a woman is weak. A woman can come and be changed easily. You will come and change her mind and she may go into your religion. That is why we prohibit our girls from going outside our religion to people of other religions."

"If that is the case, why do you take my daughter when you may go and change her religion and that of her children to become Muslim? Now, when I want your daughter, why don't you allow me to try to give her my own religion? And if she converts to my religion, it is her decision."

It is difficult.

Deng Riny, in the interview with Albino Akot, also spoke of religion:

Religion divides people; even in front of God it divides people. What it means is that people seem to indicate that their God is more important than the God of other people. I think this is where there will be a problem. When people come and say, "Our God is more important than your God," that is when trouble comes.

Unless this question of religion is solved, people may be in contact but one person will have his own way and the other person will have his own way. They will both say, "We are brothers," but each man will know deep inside his heart that they are different.

Chief Thon Wai comments on the difficulties working against integration, specifying Arab prejudice as the main obstacle.

Today, the Sudan is united. It has become one. Nobody will separate it. But there is still something that will divide it. What will divide it is the sort of thing I was saying. If we are truly one, why is it that we do not marry Arab girls? He keeps his girl from us totally. And our girl he marries. He has been taking our girls, beginning with the sisters of our grandfathers and our fathers. What we do not like is this division. We say that we are one people and then divide ourselves over religion. I say that if people do not accept one another to intermarry, then religion is not going to unite us. Religion is the word of God. And we are one people in front of God.

If we keep refusing one another because of religion, the single God will be divided into two. We are all part of one God. The man who prays in the Muslim tradition is praying to God; and the man who does not pray in the Muslim way but prays in another way is also praying to God. If we do not intermarry, we are not one; if we really want to be one, we have to intermarry.

While most of the Dinka attack Arab prejudice on the issue

of marriage, they do not refer to their own prejudice against
intermarriage with the Arabs, which they confess only when
pushed to state the attitude of their people about mixed
marriages. Chief Biong bases his argument against intermarriage with the Arabs on the Arab's basic prejudice and
what he considers Arab disdain even of in-law relationship
with the Dinka. His own prejudice, however, comes through.

> We cannot tell a lie and say that we will become one
> people with these Arabs. These people, how can we inter-
> marry with them? The women he takes from us are
> slaves. The Arabs do not marry many wives. They marry
> only two wives legally and then have slaves. And where
> do these slaves come from? They are from our part of
> the country. Even if we were to intermarry with them,
> they will marry our girls only to be their slaves. And if
> a war should break out between us, the Arab will kill his
> own maternal relatives and his own relatives-in-law. He
> would not care. The Dinka cannot enter a relationship
> with such a person.

Chief Makuei Bilkuei was more direct in his admission of
Dinka prejudice. Asked whether the Dinka would accept
intermarriage with the Arabs, he said:

> No, they will not; they will never accept. Only women
> who get attracted by money will accept. Those are the
> ones with whom they have intercourse. Otherwise the
> Dinka will never accept. They attract only the women of
> the town. Our Dinka women will never do it.

Chief Albino Akot draws a distinction between the educated and the traditional Dinka; the former might adapt to
mixed marriages, the latter would be surely opposed to it.

> Well, with the Dinka it may depend. The educated class
> may have varying ideas. Some may like the mixture,
> some may not. But for those who are totally uneducated

and who are not concerned with town life or with the educated class, the bulk of the Dinka—they would not like it. Never. They will never appreciate the mixture. They are different. It is impossible.

And according to Deng Riny, the Dinka are just as prejudiced as the Arabs.

Dinkas see themselves as superior. The idea of somebody else being above him is not known to the Dinka. They think they are the people created best. So from the point of view of Dinka feelings too, the Dinka will resist intermarriage; they will resist integration. The idea of an Arab coming and marrying among the Dinka will not be accepted.

Each man sees himself as superior. The Arabs see themselves as superior and the Dinka see themselves as superior. In this case it is difficult to see how they will mix. But if people become equal so that there is no poor and there is no rich, and Arabs do not see the Dinka as poor and the Dinka do not see the Arabs as inferiors, then they could approach one another as equals.

In the view of Chief Yusuf Deng, himself a Muslim, intermarriage is a personal matter which education and opportunities for contact will solve; it is not a political issue between the North and the South.

What about those girls and boys who were in the field today performing together, are they all from one area? They are children who have grown up together. There were Southerners among them and there were Northerners among them. They will come to know each other by themselves. So the issue of marriage is not going to affect us. It should be left to the educated youth to settle; it is their own case.

Education has mixed people up; they are writing together; they are going to school together. People in the same class, what they will say amongst themselves no one knows. So, the question of marriage, I think, will work itself out by itself. We will not make it a problem. A man will like a girl and marry her according to their own feelings.

Chief Lino Aguer had a similar view of the situation:

What will change all this is education. For instance, girls of white people have been brought to this country. They have been brought here because of education. So tomorrow, when our girls are educated, they will do it their way. For instance, some girls are sent to Juba for education. They come to love their colleagues and say, "This man I want him to marry me." So, this kind of thing, who will lay it down as a law? The Sudan cannot put it down as a law. It is education which will solve it.

My thoughts about marriage are two. Intermarriage will come in two ways, I think. One way is our way, we in the South; the way a person lives in his own culture and the way his girls have always been married. The people who would marry in that way are known. Another way is the way of education. What will happen because of education seems to be different and lies ahead in the future. For instance, a man goes and finds his own wife in a different place. A Dinka girl may be found by a man from another area, whether it is Ndogo or Jur Col or Zande. They marry with money. They may go and meet during their education and agree among themselves. The word of the father will then come later on. Will he allow his daughter to be married with money? If he accepts, then he has accepted the word of education; he will have followed the way of education. If he does not accept, then he has refused the way of education and he has endorsed the way of the Dinka. No law will force him.

The question of education comes in the heart of each man: the way he sees it, the way it influences him. I cannot really say that this way is going to affect everybody, to fuse the blood of everybody. It is the way that education works within each person which shows whether you will marry a girl for money or for cattle. It is the way education has actually influenced your thinking and that of the girl and that of the girl's father. I do not think we can do it by law and say that we have become one and that we have to mix and marry. I think it would be wrong to say that a girl who has not accepted a non-Dinka will be given to a non-Dinka, a Dor, or an Arab, or that an Arab girl who does not want a Dinka will be forced to marry a Dinka.

Commenting on the high-value bridewealth among the Dinka which deters other people from intermarrying with the Dinka and on the prospects for its reduction, Lino said:

Goods are sold according to where they come from. The goods in the shop are sold according to where they came from and how they were made and how they were bought. If you bought the goods for a lot of cattle, you want a little profit; you want just a little more to go on top of what you had paid. Among the Dinka, marriage is not decided by chiefs; it is a question of those who have goods—those people who have the girls.

Girls are goods to them. Their mothers were married with cattle. They are given away in the same way their mothers were married. A man will see his daughter, notice how long she has stayed without being married, wonder whether she is not married because the price is high. If so, then he will put it down. When he sees that his goods are not being sold because of the high price, he will lower it. So that will be determined by the father of the girl.

According to Deng Riny, elaborating a point introduced earlier, it is the elimination of poverty and the achievement of social equality that will remove prejudice against mixed marriages.

> What we really want is a way to destroy this question of poverty among our people. Cattle are no longer the source of wealth. It has now become money which is the source of wealth and therefore, from that point of view, our people are poor. It is by eliminating poverty that we can bring an equality which will help in bringing our people closer together.
>
> If I have wealth, you can come and mix with me in the evening and therefore we become relatives. But if I do not have anything, then it is difficult for you to come to me.
>
> If you are wealthy and you are a man of position, even if you are not a Muslim, they can give you their daughter. It is only if you are inferior to them materially that they will of course not want to give their daughter to you. What they want is what you have and that can easily change their attitude. Basically, disrespect comes from the fact that you have nothing, not just from your race. When they say, "Of what value are you?" it means that you are poor. When each has his own power, then people can respect one another. It is just like strong bulls. When bulls are both strong, they respect one another and avoid fighting.

Views on the prospects of integration within the South envision obstacles similar to those presented on the issue of South-North integration, but with greater desire for the goals and less dogmatism on the obstacles. For instance, Chief Makuei, who was so dogmatic about how the Dinka would oppose intermarriage with the North, had this to say about integration within the South: "What I told you about sharing the meat we slaughter is the important thing between us and the North; but we on this side, we should not divide it and divide it and divide it and say, 'There is this section and that section.' That would spoil it."

Asked how the Dinka would react to mixed marriage with non-Dinka Southerners, Chief Makuei concedes that it will be difficult for the Dinka to give their daughters to non-Dinkas but he believes it may happen in the long run.

> Yes, it will be difficult with such people as the daughters of the Jok and the daughters of the Twic, and the daughters of the Rek. These are women now in the cattle-byres using ashes on their skins. What will change it is a long way away; it is a long way away. People who eat wild plants in the forest cannot really meet with the Twic, with the Rek, indeed with all the Dinka. Their ways are different. I don't see how they can change easily; it is a long way away.

Lino Aguer, however, retained his original stand on the issue of intermarriage even within the Southern groups.

> It is the same in the South. In the South today, even of a Rek who speaks the same language as you, some people may say, "My daughter will not go that far." There are people who still say that. You know that the word against marrying a non-Dinka is even stronger. Some people have now come as far as here [Juba]. Some Dinka have married Dor girls and some Dor have married Dinka girls. What has done it is education and not custom or law. What you accept by education is simpler, but what is forced onto your head never works.

Chief Giirdit draws a distinction between intermarriage with the other Nilotics like the Nuer and the Shilluk on the one hand and the rest of the "Sudanic" peoples like the Azande and the Ndogo on the other hand. The former poses no significant problems.

> Your problem with the Nuer is easy because you are one people. There is no problem, you are one. The Nuer and the Dinka are the sons of the same father and the same mother. And as for the Shilluk and the Jur Col, they are the children of Amou. Therefore they are our maternal relatives.

In Chief Giirdit's view, the latter is more formidable: "But I think that the issue of the Dor will be even more difficult. It will be difficult for you people to intermarry with the Dor."

But according to Akol, who argued with Giirdit about the question of integration in general and intermarriage in particular: "There is really no way of controlling the mixing of people. Unless we lock people inside, as long as people get outside and mix with others, there will be young men who will meet with Arab girls and non-Dinka girls and intermarry."

In one interview with the Ngok elders there was a sharp difference of opinion which indicated the cleavage between the traditional Dinka view that would oppose intermarriage and the emerging view that recognizes the present impact and future implications of the current interaction and mutual assimilation among diverse ethnic and cultural elements in the Sudan. According to Marieu Ajak, expressing the latter view:

> As I see it, in the future of our world ahead, I think we shall marry Arab girls and I believe the Arabs will marry our girls. The country wants to mix and it is already beginning to mix. We shall be one. Our girls used to refuse Arabs in the past. Today, they accept them. As I see it, our children too, if a boy likes an Arab girl, he will be

allowed to marry her. An Arab who likes a Dinka girl will marry her. Our girls do not carry pens, but they have had children with Arabs. In court, a girl would be told "There is your man, a Dinka," but she would refuse and go with an Arab policeman or with an ordinary Arab from the merchants we have at Abyei. I believe our country has become one and, as I see it, we shall intermarry in the future.

Chol Adija expressed the opposite view:

What kind of marriages do you say exist now? Marriages with prostitutes? Have you seen any decent girl, a daughter of a gentleman, marrying an Arab? . . . We, the Ngok have remained away from the black peoples of the South for very long. This is what your father used to say. That is why going to the South is difficult for us. But we intermarry with our people in the South. Many are the descendants of the daughters of the Twic and the Rek, starting from your family of Deng Kwol. But from the Arabs we have not married even a single girl. And he does not marry from us either. All he can get from us are the prostitutes he searches for in Abyei town. But a marriage, as that the daughter of so and so is married, exists only between us and the Ruweng and the Nuer—if we find a girl—and the Pan Aruu. But we do not intermarry with these people here.

As may be quite apparent, Chol Adija, like Chief Giirdit, represents tradition, and his companions, like Akol in the interview with Giirdit, represent change. This cleavage reflects age differences, even though this is more evident in Giirdit's interview and less marked in the Ngok interview. It also seems apparent that the forces of change have a strong case against the forces of tradition and that much of what is now happening tends to support change.

This change is indeed reflected in the degree to which the

Dinka, despite the intensification of their negative view of the Arab, have now begun to identify with a wider world beyond their own. Throughout the interviews we encountered a recurrent theme of identification with the black world, which suggests that their nationalistic aspirations have been enormously extended on ethnic, racial, or cultural lines. This nationalistic consciousness is, however, an emotionalized conceptual reaction to what they view as a Northern Arab ethnocentric attitude toward them, especially as manifested in the post-colonial policies of assimilation along Arab-Islamic lines, and to other inequities in the sharing of all material and spiritual values. Proud and ethnocentric as the Dinka themselves are, they become more obsessed with other people's prejudices against them and the need for eliminating those prejudices than they are conscious of their own subjectivities and prejudices. This is a plaintiff psychology which recognition, equality, and shared responsibility can help mitigate in the interest of the common good. And that is precisely what the solution of the Southern problem seems to be doing, although its impact has not yet become sufficiently absorbed to be adequately reflected as part of the Dinka pattern of thought and behavior.

5. Conclusion

In this book, I have tried to substantiate from interview materials the Dinka conception of their world: their place in the "Original Byre of Creation," their struggle for survival in a hostile environment, and the prospects for their contribution to the building of a modern Sudanese nation.

Their myths of creation, original leadership, and early migration, which they recount in great detail and with vivid imagination and consistency, reveal striking resemblances to the classic books of Middle Eastern religions. As these myths were told by elderly people, who claim to have heard them from their fathers and grandfathers, they could not have been adapted from the twentieth-century missionary influence in the area. Instead, the myths suggest that the Dinka must have had early contacts with their neighbors in the Northern Sudan and the Middle East. This is not surprising and should indeed be implicit in the observations of anthropologists who, though not possessing the material produced here, assert that the religious beliefs and practices of the Dinka and their cultural kindred, the Nuer, are reminiscent of these classic Middle Eastern religions. The common features between the Nilotics and their Northern neighbors have indeed been said to extend into other cultural areas and to be reflected in the racial admixture of both the North and the South.

This lack of a clear-cut dichotomy in the cultural or racial composition of the Sudan should have been a positive basis for unity and nation-building, but instead, political history has not only tended to conceal it from both the Southerner and the Northerner, but has emphasized the divisive elements and fostered a sense of mistrust and animosity. Much of this has been based on the bitter memory of the nineteenth-century upheavals which predated the advent of colonial rule and which was subsequently fanned, especially in the South, to help impede the rise of united nationalism. Also divisive have been the post-colonial hostilities of the civil war which again focused devastation and suffering on the Southern people and nursed in them a deep sense of grievance against their Northern countrymen.

The negative view of the past is strongly voiced and substantiated by the accounts of the chiefs and elders but is sharply contrasted with the highly commendable way the South-North civil war was recently ended, and the peace and unity that have resulted from the settlement. This contrasting combination has given the Dinka a complex perspective which, though embittered by memory of the past, is also responsive to the positive gestures of the present, yet apprehensive and even pessimistic about the future prospects. Deeply wounded by past experience, many Dinkas cannot believe that the Northerner has truly changed and that he will continue to make the necessary adjustments in his attitude toward the Southerners to consolidate and guarantee lasting peace and unity. Some chiefs and elders consider the agreement the outcome of divine wisdom on the part of President Nimeri as an exceptional Northerner, and view it as a tenuous compromise and an interim arrangement that should lead to separation as the ultimate solution.

But these are the voices of injured men, reflecting an inward outlook that is hardly aware of the surrounding dynamics and constraints. The subtleties with which leaders in the North have been restructuring the political process across the South-North dividing line, their increasing self-discovery as Afro-Arab, not essentially different from or superior to the Southerners, their genuineness in extending a conciliatory hand to the South, and above all the forces favoring unity on the national, regional, and international levels are all conditioning factors which the chiefs and elders do not adequately consider in predicting the future.

Nevertheless, their bitter view of the past, their appreciation of the present settlement, and their grim vision of the future are remnants of a deep-rooted reaction to a tragic human experience that must be recognized to be effectively erased. It is quite understandable that the accounts of the chiefs and elders do not sufficiently reflect the conciliatory mood that has emerged because, when I conducted the interviews in 1972, the peace settlement, which marks the conspicuous turning point of a positive evolution that had been in the making over a period of decades, had only just been achieved. The conflict was still fresh in the minds of those interviewed. Indeed, the stronger the bitter voice of the South about past hostilities, the more one realized the magnitude of the problem that had to be overcome in achieving peace and unity, the greater the appreciation of this achievement, and the deeper the insight into what is still required to create an atmosphere conducive to lasting peace and unity. Indeed, contemporary experience is beginning to reveal new dimensions and insights into the history of conflict in the area and is indicating that some positive lessons could be drawn from the recurrent suffering, endurance, and continued readiness of the people to face the challenges of survival with determination and optimism. Sudanese on both sides are rapidly overcoming the hatred of seventeen years' insurgence, and though perhaps not forgetting the agony of the civil war and earlier conflicts, are living up to the moral and material challenge of reconciliation and solidarity in nation-building.

One must therefore distinguish between the chiefs' factual accounts of the past hostilities, their pessimistic subjective assessments of the future—conditioned as they are by these hostilities—and a scientific prediction that places South-North relations in a broader context characterized by the dynamics of modern nation-building. There is no disagreement over the past. The prejudices are both understandable and relevant but the dynamics of nation-building, though complex and fraught with dangers, are nonetheless evolving toward consolidating peace and unity. Indeed, they have already helped promote the stability necessary for development and even attracted the financial means and technical know-how essential to international cooperation in development. In addition, they have enabled the Sudan to actively play out its long-postulated Afro-Arab role of linkage, mediation, and conciliation.

For a long time this constructive role was largely a potential, emanating from the dualistic character of the Sudan as both Arab and African. For the same reason, it was debilitated by the South-North conflict and the reverse of the postulate was the reality. In the face of what was popularly perceived as an Arab-African civil war, the Sudan became a divisive factor within the continent and in the relations of the Africans and the Arabs. The history of the country from its beginning to its present and in its projection into the future was conceived in terms of the conflict and its implications. The Sudan being a microcosm of Africa in its ethnic and cultural diversities, this grim image of Afro-Arab relations was reflected at all levels within and beyond the continent, even though aspirations about Sudan's constructive potential continued to rival the negative reality.

So dominant was the perspective of conflict that the obvious racial and cultural complexities and admixtures of the country were hardly acknowledged. Indeed, they were often denied and the South and the North were conceived as having been always racially and culturally distinct and mutually opposed. What was more, no one saw a solution in view. Africa remained committed to the maintenance and respect of the borders inherited from colonial powers and the outside world was incapacitated by Africa's jealous guarding of the newly won independence and its militant opposition to any interference in the domestic affairs of African nations. The result was that in the heart of Africa, within a country bordering eight nations—the largest on the continent—an internecine war of grave magnitude remained rampant while the eyes of the international community at best remained lowered in embarrassment.

In addition to its destruction of life and property and its divisiveness in the face of demands for nation-building, the conflict caused economic devastation and retardation of development. And needless to say, the resultant instability deterred foreign investment.

But for the same reason that the conflict was an embarrassment, the peace settlement was a cause for pride and universal rejoicing. Domestically, the settlement has generated a new positive mood which has encouraged a more complex appreciation of identifying symbols. This has resulted in a stabilizing restructuring of interest groups that makes the South-North dichotomy a less divisive feature. Furthermore, the principles of social justice underlying the granting of autonomy and the implicit wider shaping and sharing of political power have ensured a broader based interest-identification with the system. So have the massive development programs which largely aim at adjusting the urban-rural imbalances that previous plans created through emphasis on the relatively more developed areas, where the infrastructure was sufficiently advanced to attract investment. The alliance of the working forces has meant recognizing as political constituencies a large variety of interest groups—including the military, professionals, industrial workers, farmers, the business community, the parent-teacher association, women, youth, and the intelligentsia—all of whom are represented in the Socialist Union and the People's Assembly, both regionally and nationally.

The outcome of all this is that while the Southern region

remains an autonomous entity, the political dynamics are blurring the dividing line, and instead of the South and the North being the predominant political interest groups, there has emerged a more complex system of cross-alliances, with peace, unity, stability, and development as the major rallying points. Any threat to this system means a threat to a large variety of interests united by a common cause and committed to stability. The failures of several coup attempts show that it is no longer easy to topple the system in the face of the broad-based support it now enjoys. Even if a takeover were to succeed in the North, the South would probably be a formidable defender of the system and the unity of the country, or, failing that, would almost certainly fight to break away.

But while in my view the South is committed to the stability of the system and the unity of the country, the nature of the established autonomy is rather complex and entails a delicate balance between peace, unity, and autonomy. The achievement of peace was possible because the principle of national unity was recognized as paramount, but the principle of unity itself was accepted because autonomy was granted to the South. Unity continues to be postulated not only as desired but as achieved. But the Southerners are also jealously guarding their autonomy and are quick to see and resent anything that might approximate a violation of the Addis Ababa Agreement. This naturally poses a threat to the achieved peace and unity, but the North is conscious of that and is minimizing its involvement in the South. Nevertheless, Southerners participate on both the regional and the central levels with a degree of dependency on the center. There are still questions as to the relative emphasis the Southerners will place on their participation in the center or the region in the future and what that is likely to mean in terms of consolidating the achieved unity and promoting national integration of diversity and discrepancies which have been divisive obstacles to nation-building.

The acceptance of diversity in unity is of course the cornerstone of the present South-North relations, but in view of the harmonious interaction peace has ensured between them and the hierarchical nature of the dual regional-central participation of the South, we can expect the process to result in some political, cultural, and ethnic integration of the country. Of course, this is certain to entail a give-and-take on both sides, but the precise proportions would depend on a number of considerations, including the vitality of the elements contributed and the declared policy position in support of the competing symbols of identity and the degree to which they do not overtly threaten other important competitive symbols. It is noticeable, for instance, that after peace was achieved and Southern autonomy established, the concept of Arabism ceased to be repressive to the South and therefore became less sensitive or divisive. Indeed, while the issue of identity continues to be debatable and controversial, there is a wide acceptance of the Afro-Arab dualism of Sudanese identity and a positive utilization of both concepts in the interest of the country and its conciliatory role in regional and international affairs. The contribution of the Arab world to the development efforts of the Sudan has been pivotal in this conciliatory view of identity and might well continue to be a significant determinant in the ultimate outcome of integration. In many ways, the process is reminiscent of the vital role played by trade in facilitating the Afro-Arab integration of the Northern Sudan.

This economic perspective is indeed worth emphasizing for, as I have already indicated, one of the most conspicuous features of the recent development, not only in South-North relations but in the whole country, is the manner with which the government has succeeded in making development fill the vacuum that the end of the war might have created with regard to where the attention of the people was directed. As the accounts show, even the traditional people now display a surprising and indeed obsessive commitment to development. Contrary to the popular conception of chiefs as agents of conservatism and resistance to development, they portray and defend themselves as a dynamic potential for facilitating development. Regionally and internationally, the attention of the world is focused on the enormous agricultural resources of the Sudan, comprising some 200 million acres of arable land of which only 17 million acres are currently utilized, and the role the Sudan could play as the breadbasket of the Middle East and a contributor of needed food to help alleviate the impending crises of hunger in the world. Nor is agriculture the only potential. Livestock, minerals, forestry, fishery, and even oil are competitors for development, although the Sudan has clearly defined its priority for agricultural development. Many Arab countries have shown their interest in assisting the Sudan in this field, and the newly established Arab Authority for Agricultural Investment and Development has chosen the Sudan for its headquarters and as its first recipient model. The industrial world, both governmental and corporate, is also responding to the Sudanese appeal for development cooperation. Their response often includes an appreciation of the domestic achievements of the Sudan, especially in the establishment of peace, unity, and stability, and also support of the constructive role the country is expected to play in international relations. They recognize and appreciate the fact that the Sudan has enacted appropriate legislation to create a climate conducive to private investment, domestic and foreign.

This massive domestic and international commitment to the development of the Sudan does not necessarily guarantee a balanced improvement in the material, moral, and spiritual quality of life for the masses of the people in the traditional sector of the country. As anyone concerned with the development process in the third world will realize, to accelerate modernization in traditional societies usually implies the paradox of enriching the people with technological advantages while seriously disrupting their social and moral order with grave disintegrating, and perhaps dehumanizing, consequences. What is needed is a model that would balance the need for technological advancement against the importance of preserving what is best in the pre-modernization social context of the people, including their values and social institutions. Indeed, the challenge is more than a negative one of counteracting the adverse effects of change; it should positively aim at facilitating development by creatively building on the human and cultural resources of the pre-modernization context. It is now generally agreed that development plans often fail and vast resources get wasted because of failure to understand the social context and to adopt appropriate measures that would both minimize the negatives and facilitate the acceptance of development and the contribution of the local people.

Of course, despite the increasing universal concern with this problem, no one has found the solution and the Sudan is no exception. Abundant evidence in the accounts of the chiefs illustrates the magnitude of the problem, even when the people involved may not be well aware of it. In fact, much of the history of Dinka suffering has directly or indirectly resulted from ill-planned, misguided, or unguided change, the consequences of which have been disruption and disintegration, with few if any positive counterbalances. But the Sudan's current approach to development, which emphasizes social justice and welfare in rural and community development, and the importance of self-help both in promoting development and fostering a sense of worth in the people, is a significant trend in the positive direction. Considering the vast quantity of arable land in the Sudan, it should be possible to maximize production by adopting large-scale mechanization of agriculture over massive stretches of land, and also to help the small farmer to improve his agricultural techniques through the adoption of small-scale mechanized techniques. Another significant asset in the Sudan's approach to development is the emphasis being given to an equitable distribution of services, especially in the health and educational fields. This means laying stress on the delivery of essential medical services through paramedical staff. Sophisticated medical services by highly trained professionals are of course not to be disregarded, but should be an exception and practiced in a facility for both treatment and training, while the primary concern remains at the grassroots level. Equally, a great portion of the educational resources are being devoted to lower- and middle-school training, even though high-level academic orientation remains valued and should contribute to research on and better understanding of the problems of development and their solutions.

All these efforts have been launched only recently and their results are not yet visible. Unfortunately in most countries, the Sudan included, positive developments in one area may not be well coordinated with needs in other areas, and therefore remain unknown, unappreciated, and unutilized. This is particularly the case with the gap between research and application. Much of the sensitivity to the extra-economic dimensions of development is found in universities and research centers, rarely extending into the field or the village. What is needed then is an integrated approach that extends the services of universities and research institutions into the community and conversely returns to these institutions any new challenges emanating from the field experience. The National Research Council, the newly established Institute for Development Studies of the University of Khartoum, the Universities of the Gezira and Juba which are being established, and the envisaged Arid Zone Research Institute are all aimed at furthering this interplay between research, application, and community service.

One concrete example will illustrate the importance of sensitivity to the social context and its material and moral contribution to development. The age-set system is a vital military, economic, social, and psychological institution among the Dinka. Once initiated in their mid-teens, young men are then affiliated into a corporate unit whose role is primarily to defend the society against human and animal foes, but also is involved in such economic activities as distant herding and in all other activities in which physical strength and courage are necessary. The competitiveness of age-sets as representatives of tribal units is an important motivating factor in their functions. During the British period, age-sets were effectively utilized in building roads, schools, dispensaries, and other public buildings as well as cultivating public agricultural fields. They soon adopted this public service as a symbol of the manhood challenge implicit in the age-set system. In their competitiveness, age-sets tried to excel and in their war songs, in which they allege to be stronger than their enemies or opponents, they began to sing about competition in public service. Age-sets bragged of themselves as "the bulls," "the lions," or the warriors who endured the hardships of public service while the weaklings remained in the comfort of the home amidst women. Even the speed with which the job was done was a factor in the pride of the age-set. As the amount of road mileage was allocated on tribal grounds, competition extended to the level of larger political units and, as some of the interviews indicate, the chiefs competed through their age-set in performance of this public service. After independence, this form of public service was abolished as forced labor. Since tribal warfare is no longer an accepted practice, this has left the age-set with little or no corporate incentive and, although initiation is still practiced, the dynamic character of the age-set system is waning. In some areas initiation has indeed been abolished with no creative attempts at substitutes. Where it is still practiced, young men now leave immediately after initiation and flock to urban centers where they become domestic servants or occupy other menial jobs which relegate them to the lowest levels of the urban stratum, with all the psychological implications such a stratification implies. Thus, in sharp contrast to a practice which built on the human, moral, and psychological resources of a traditional institution to promote a locally oriented dignifying development, a disintegrating and dehumanizing model of development was introduced.

But of course Dinka traditional society and the modern context into which it has merged constitute a complexity of paradoxes and there can be no easy model for the social problems, old or new. As the Dinka said in the interviews, the most prudent attitude toward the post–civil war situation is to wait and see in order to determine how real or lasting all the positive indications are. Nevertheless, since I conducted the interviews there has been enough evidence to justify optimism. After more than five years of careful adherence to the spirit and the letter of the Addis Ababa peace settlement between the North and the South, it is time for relative relaxation and a reexamination of the history of the Southern peoples and their relations to the North. Viewed positively, there is much in the sociological history of the Dinka to draw upon in the constructive task of nation-building. With the worldwide support that the domestic achievements of peace, unity, and development now enjoy and the tripartite development cooperation this support promises, there is reason to be optimistic about the future. Manageable realism, positive orientation, and constructive utilization of opportunities have always been vital in the Dinka heritage.

Index